THIRD EDITION

SHIFT

THE TRANSFER OF WEALTH

SUCCESSFUL ENTREPRENEURS & PASTORS
DR. RAYMOND & DEBORAH LARSON

7 DEGREES

SHIFT—the transfer of wealth

Printed in the United States of America
4th Printing August 2018

ISBN: 978-1-7289609-6-8

Please note that the author's publishing style may capitalize certain pronouns in Scripture that refer to the Father, God, Son, and the Holy Spirit, and may differ from some publisher's styles. We have deliberately chosen not to capitalize the word satan or related terms even though it may violate grammatical rules. Other personal emphasis may also violate grammatical rules, and are done so by intention.

To Contact the Authors

www.7Degrees.org

DEDICATION

This book is dedicated to David Russet, friend,
mentor, and lover of Christ, who modeled the
kingdom of God in his personal and public life.

And, to Raymond's grandfather, Mike Lawrence,
who understood and was successful in the marketplace
better than most, and yet he never
graduated from the ninth grade.

To many, who taught Deborah how to walk in the Spirit,
hear the heartbeat of the Father, stand firm without waveri'
and cheered her on, "Thank you, great is your reward!'

Finally, to those who have lived the life of Priest an'
unnoticed or unappreciated, and have waiter'
this season of promotion and realignme
We honor your sacrifices, diligence, and 4r
journey you have traveled by example. T
day and time; the transfer is awai†

ENDORSEMENTS

"I have known Raymond Larson for over 25 years when he was senior pastor at Bethel Church in Redding California. He is a seasoned veteran in God's army and after all these years He serves, loves, and ministers to people with the excellence of the Kingdom of God. If you don't know him, just give him a few minutes and the anointing of Christ that is in this chosen vessel will fill your heart and you will be blessed, encouraged, and equipped for the work of the Lord. It is an honor for me to know and recommend this book to you."

GEORGIAN BANOV
President and Co-founder of Global Celebration

"As a 25-year marketplace veteran and mentor of the next generation, I have been waiting for such a book to be published. This is the time when all of God's people should be refining their skills through the Word of God by the examples of those who have paved the way. Tracking with "Generals" of the faith, and learning the culture of heaven here on earth is not only a dream, but is being done every day by people like you and me. How God's people handle His provision is essential—especially navigating through increasingly tough times.

To Dr. Raymond and Deborah Larson, I say thank you! You have truly heard from heaven. It is easy to recognize when God has found someone He can trust with a word for the masses, and it's proven evident by the facts, the fruit, and the testimony in this book. SHIFT—The Transfer of Wealth, is a must-read. This book is not only a testimony of real-life experiences that has been exciting to read, but also a simple blueprint that, when applied and walked out, will not only change your life, but the lives of those around you. Do you want more? If you do, or know someone who would like to experience victory in their lives in a fresh and easy-to-understand way, this book will put you on track. It's time to be excited when you wake up on a Monday morning, knowing that God is going to use you to make a difference!

JOHN W. ARNTSEN
Entrepreneur, Business Owner

"This is a real story that brings understanding to the mysteries of God's design for your life—specifically—why you just lived through all the unexplainable events that you experienced. It pieces together seemingly unrelated life experiences and decades of theological mysteries.

I have lived this journey and from a non-religious perspective. God promises that His words never fall to the ground. All the parts weave together when you stay above circumstance and remember He does the work when you walk in sync with His heart and character. This book is not for philosophers, navel-gazers or legalists. It was written for those who want to understand the heart of the Father and are ready to accept their new assignments."

DEBORAH LARSON
Wife, Mom, Grandmother,
Daughter & Pursuer of His Presence

A C K N O W L E D G E M E N T S

Deborah and I would first like to thank Nyla Marks, who has always believed in, supported, and shown the character of Christ to us. Your actions went beyond words, and in the moment when you feel that no one noticed, we did. Enjoy heaven, we shall see you soon!

Mark Hinman, who was Raymond's first pastor, and who instilled in him a dynamic sense of the presence and purpose of God. You loved well!

Jim Lillard, our dear friend who is with Jesus, you are one of the few men who understand Kingdom finance, provision, and how to be a friend of God. Thanks for the friendship.

To our brother Ron Rasmussen, whom I honor, love, and am most grateful to the Lord for more than I can write on this page. To Deborah's mom, Edwina L. Wright, all that you ever aspired for your daughter, God has kept His word beyond your wildest dreams. Enjoy Jesus until we meet you there. Finally, to our children, grandchildren, and yours: The reason we are passionate about establishing a generational blessing and transfer of Heaven's resources. And, last but surely not least, to our Lord Jesus Christ, for whom we stand speechless, astounded and overwhelmed at the fulfillment of promises He has made. All glory, honor, and recognition is due, only to you!

C O N T E N T S

PREFACE   XV

FOREWORD   XVII

INTRODUCTION   XXI

PART ONE—A MASS IN MOTION

CHAPTER ONE   1
A GLIMPSE OF WHAT'S TO COME

1	The Mountain Calls Out
5	A Heart Preparation for Acceleration
6	An Unplanned Exit
8	Courage and Character
10	The Pressure Cooker Continues
12	Revelation in the Fourth Watch
14	History Records the Glory
18	A Key in Victories to Come: Remember!
20	The Storehouse Released

CHAPTER TWO   23
THE LORD BREAKS OUT BEFORE ME

23	The Adventure Grows
26	A Strange Phone Call
27	The Father's Laughter
30	The Water Breaks Forth
32	The Wealth of Influence
34	The Increase of An Open Heaven
36	Stones Laid With Purpose
37	Back to The Future
38	For Today and Tomorrow

CHAPTER THREE   39
A MANDATE OF FULFILLMENT

39	His Original Intentions
43	His Plan—An Aerial View
45	A Change in Operating Systems
47	A Personal *Shift*
50	No Thank You, Dr. Schofield
51	There is Only One Exit Strategy
52	The *Shift* Has Begun
52	A Realignment in You

CHAPTER FOUR   55
HIS STOREHOUSE FOR TRANSFER

55	His Original Intentions
56	Warning! A Loss in Translation
57	The Power of Words
60	Forfeiting Your Inheritance
62	Unused Heavenly Resources
63	A Legal Right
64	An Inside Perspective

CHAPTER FIVE 67
CRITICAL MASS

67	Scientific Proof and Supernatural Truth
68	A Moment of Change
70	*Shift* Factors ...
71	A Keen Sense for the Obvious
74	On a Colliding Path
76	He Who Owns the Gold Makes the Rules
80	Doused With Cold Water
82	Moving in Motion with Him
84	Perfect Timing
85	Accelerated Movement
86	Soaring With Extraordinary Momentum

GALLERY OF PHOTOS 89

PART TWO—REALIGNMENT: A GENERATIONAL ORDER

CHAPTER SIX 101
THE CONTAINER STORE®

101	A Personal Fit
102	Value of The Vessels ... Inside Out
105	Vessels to Reveal His Glory
108	Dirty Water Wine
111	An Unending Supply
113	The Holy Container—You!
115	Overflowing Containers

CHAPTER SEVEN   117
STEWARDING THE SHIFT

117   A Dramatic Wake-Up Call
119   Defining Roles
120   In the Beginning
121   Stewardship Vs. Ownership
124   God's Intellectual Properties
126   Loosen Your Grip!
129   Good Stewardship Defined
133   *Shift* Happens, Now What?

CHAPTER EIGHT   137
FINANCED TO OCCUPY

137   His Nation—Occupy 'til I Come
140   Nation, Tribe, And Family
141   His Plan … Individually
143   How Do I Get There?
145   Skin In The Game … Yours
146   When Success Factors Turn Downward
149   Can I Not Give it Back to You in a Day?
151   His Return on Your Investment
152   What About the Benjamin's?
154   Who Is Your Daddy?
154   It's All About the Money
157   Positioned For Transfer

CHAPTER NINE   161
CONVERGING ANOINTING

162   Kings and Priests—A New Consideration
166   History of the Church

168   Displacement of Kings—Elevating Priests
171   Repentance to The Kings
174   The New Temple—A Finished Reformation
177   A Many Stranded Chord
180   The Formidable Force of Unity

CHAPTER TEN   183
THE PERFECT STORM

183   A Runway for the Bride—Not a Runaway Bride
185   When Convergence Happens
185   Making Money is Holy
188   Facing Outward
190   A Fivefold *Shift*
191   When Kings Go With Blessing
192   Joint Venture with God
194   A Cadence March
195   Unleashing His Provision
200   His Overflow of Abundance

CHAPTER ELEVEN   203
AFTER YOUR TRANSFER

203   In it For the Long Haul
204   Surprise! More Than You Could Imagine
208   Provision for Generational Inheritance
210   Your Plan—Write it Down
213   Spreading His Wealth
215   Partnerships and Protégé
217   Profitability: A Mutual Alliance

CHAPTER TWELVE 221
DOMINION AUTHORITY

221   A Daily Mandate
222   The Lord's Prayer
222   Part One: Reproducing The Kingdom
223   Part Two: Daily Attitudes To Sustain Victory
225   Transfer to Transformation

ENDNOTES 229

RAYMOND & DEBORAH LARSON 233

PREFACE

This is not another Christian book to create anticipation and hope without evidence available to prove it. It's not another futuristic prophetic glimpse of what is to come. This book is for the NOW. It is written for the children of God to ready themselves and *immediately* participate in a great adventure prepared in Heaven for this generation. I might add that those who are to live this *Shift* have already been on the Potter's wheel being formed into the vessel that can genuinely house and intelligently steward the resources of Heaven's storehouse.

Have you ever heard quoted, "the wealth of the sinner is laid up for the righteous"? Did you contemplate how could that happen for you? It may feel like a theory rather than a living reality, until it happens. When it does, in a moment your entire life changes. We intend to show both the promise, the process and the reality of His word manifesting today; in real time. The Holy Spirit taught us about God's covenant and then allowed us to experience it first-hand.

The floodgates of Heaven are open and the Father has orchestrated the longed-for, timely access to the wealth of His storehouse. He is intentional about His Bride, His creation, and the advancement of the Kingdom that Jesus sacrificially died for. Although this book talks about money and the economy, it is merely an introduction to a spiritual yet tangible world few believe exists. Obedience, character, creative resources, and the power of Heaven are all factors, that assist you in becoming His change agent.

Here you will read what the Bible says about wealth. You will understand how His promise applies to this generation. You will observe how human events created a Critical Mass necessary for such a *Shift* to come into full force. Most importantly, the *Shift* is about God demonstrating His love for you, His creation and the true fulfillment of His Kingdom here on the earth. The Lord finances His plans and you can become the change agent who brings Him a full return. As you grow in the grace and the knowledge of Jesus Christ, your joy will not only be made full, but expand as you experience the abundance of Heaven manifest right before your eyes.

FOREWORD

When my friend Dr. Raymond Larson invited me to write the foreword for this latest book, I did not hesitate. Considering the man and the subject they are addressing, I knew something was up in the Spirit realm. Then after I read the manuscript, I knew that something important had been conceived, grown to full term, and was being birthed in the pages of this book. Raymond and Deborah have tackled a subject fraught with pitfalls, landmines, snares, religious spirits, old wives' tales, armchair quarterbacks, and back seat drivers. To have survived the process in one piece and come out on the other side is a testimony in and of itself, revealing the Lord's grace and favor. That they were able to produce the book in a concentrated and condensed period of time, is a witness of the deep work God has done in their life, the strong team around them, and their ability and sensitivity to the voice and heartbeat and gentle whispers of the Father, Son, and Spirit.

When the subject of money or wealth is mentioned, everyone has an opinion. The body of Christ is no exception. The sad reality is that those with an opinion are either dead, broke, or up to their eyeballs in debt. Most are not willing to pay the price, or endure the process, to see their dreams and destinies prove true. They opt out, burn out, go AWOL, backslide, or die without ever entering their Promised Land. They leave without defeating their giants, receiving their inheritance, or occupying the territory He had reserved for them. That cannot be said about Raymond or Deborah Larson. They have both paid the price, endured the process, and now are receiving the earthly part of the prize. It reminds me of the Scripture: "'Truly I tell you,' Jesus replied, 'no one who has left home or brothers or sisters or mother or father or children or fields for me and the Gospel will fail to receive a hundred times as much in this present age: homes, brothers, sisters, mothers, children and fields—along with persecutions—and in the age to come eternal life. But many who are first will be last, and the last first'" (Mark 10:29-31, NIV).

This book has been needed in the body of Christ for many years, as a voice of wisdom, reason and balance. We have just now entered that season of the "fullness-of-time" when convergence of the man, the message, the mantle, the Messiah, and the miracles all came together. The body of Christ is just now prepared to receive this message. The authors are right on time. The principles and process described, and documented herein have been incubated and birthed not in theory, but in practice. *This did not occur in isolation or seclusion, but on the front lines of battle.* It didn't happen in a classroom or only a boardroom, but victory occurred in the throne room of Heaven. Thus, the message contained herein has an authentic ring of truth, validated in the environment of the authors' life. The stories shared here are not enlarged, polished, or sugar-coated. Instead, they are understated, and some cases raw and unpolished. This, too adds a measure of credibility, validity and reliability to what the writer has said. In other words, the data is replicable. The principles and truths expressed here will work for anyone, anytime, in any situation, culture or environment. God is not a respecter of persons.

Moreover, the inner witness of the Spirit, and the outer witness of Scripture, provide the most convincing proofs of the book's effectiveness and lasting value. As I read through the book, I had a number of "aha" moments, when either I recognized the Holy Spirit presence or influence at work, or I recognized myself in certain stories. This told me that I had uncovered a valuable storehouse of revelation and wisdom.

As one who has been a forerunner in Kingdom marketplace, finance and stewardship for the past several years, a professional investor and consultant for 15 years, and has academically studied the history of wealth and philanthropy, I have been given a vantage point and platform to speak from. I have met and interacted with literally thousands of entrepreneurs and investors over the years, many of them self-identifying as Christians, and a fair number of theologians and thought leaders. The best way I can describe the existing state of teaching, research, and body of knowledge on the subject of wealth transfer, Kingdom stewardship and Biblical financial prosperity is "INADEQUATE" and "EXTREME." Although I can think of a dozen or two exceptions out of hundreds of books I have read on these subjects, this book, in my opinion, is destined to become a classic. So, it goes without saying that I recommend this to you for your edification, encouragement and realization.

DR. BRUCE COOK
President & Founder, The Kingdom KEYS
Vice President, Kingdom Marketplace Coalition LLC

INTRODUCTION

The word **Shift** has two (2) applications that fit what is being discussed in this book.

1. *To put (something) aside and replace it by another or others; change or exchange:*

2. *To transfer from one place, position, person, etc., to another:*

Remarkably, wealth and authority in our culture has been in the hands of those who often do not share the goals and core values our Heavenly Father's heart nor His revealed purpose for our generation. Having lived in the Priestly anointing for most of my adult life, then obeying the Holy Spirit's instructions to move into the place where Kings function, I have had the privilege of experiencing, first hand, the repositioning of finances for God's purposes through His Bride. I am living it, and I desire for lovers of God everywhere to live it as well. Kings, get ready to take your rightful place next to Priests, as we set the order for what God purposed each of us to experience. The **Shift** is gaining momentum. Get ready for, 'full speed ahead' and exhilarating power.

In the span of my forty plus years following Christ, I have heard in various ways and from an abundance of leaders that we would see the fulfillment of Proverbs 13:22b in our lifetime. You recall the often-quoted promise from Solomon's lips, *"The wealth of sinners is laid up for the righteous."* That phrase arouses a sundry of reactions along with countless interpretations. In my personal experience, I am convinced that King Solomon saw what few have comprehended. In our frail, finite thinking, we have reduced a profound declaration to a discussion on the movement of money; tragically separating camps into 'us' and 'them.'

It has been over 20 years since I first experienced the reality of this truth. As a young pastor, all I knew to do was walk in a simple, yet disciplined lifestyle. Unbeknownst to me, God had greater plans than just this experience with the transfer of His wealth as I perceived it. Thus, the title of this book: **SHIFT: The Transfer of Wealth**. Like Moses, the Holy Spirit has been teaching me, and like Moses, my long journey has seasoned and prepared me for today. The transfer is not about money. Oh, it is so much more. It is a *Shift* that has happened far too infrequently and for a shockingly few number of people. However, the floodgates of Heaven are prepared to make it the norm. This *Shift* is becoming a frequent reality to the anticipating hearts of God's children. It is a promise that must be realized for God's strategies to display a full measure of effect in our time. Make no mistake, this is the Father's earth and transformation for it is eternally in His heart. He has chosen you, but you must respond to Him with desire and passion. This *Shift* begins first on the inside. Your response determines the level of abundance God can overflow from you to others. It is time for the revealing of the Sons and Daughters of God, by the Holy Spirit's power and His purpose in us will be strategically funded by Heaven's resources. I watch with excitement the fulfillment of words the Father spoke to me, ***"The Shift has begun!"***

SHIFT

PART ONE

A MASS IN MOTION

Critical Mass is in full motion! A collision of value systems is inevitable and will occur between the Kingdom of God and our current world systems.

I propose that the prayers of the Saints filling into heaven's bowls are overflowing before the throne and demand a divine response. God is compelled to acknowledge the weight of prayer before Him, which will tip the scales on behalf of His Bride (Revelation 5).

Change is inevitable.
In what part, if any, will you
choose to participate?

CHAPTER ONE

A GLIMPSE OF WHAT'S TO COME

THE MOUNTAIN CALLS OUT

In 1987 the Father began writing on the hearts of our leadership, a need to make room for a diversity of international ministries that He was preparing to unfold. However, we were already beyond maximum amplitude in our current church facility, seating 550 people, not including children. With three service times on Sunday mornings and a consistent influx of local residents, our fellowship at Bethel Church, Redding was overflowing. There were no signs of our growth slowing down.

One day while driving up Interstate 5, I noticed a large, mesa-like hill just to the right of the intersection off of Highway 299 East. This monstrous-like mountain caught my attention, and I could not remove myself from its vantage point. It seemed to call out to me. Recognizing it was a supernatural impression that would often come to me from the Father, I veered away from my intended route to my new awaiting appointment, and I started searching for a way to get to the summit of that hill.

I discovered that there was no direct access to the property and it took me a significant amount of time to find a road leading me to a dead-end with a locked gate. That did not stop my pursuit, as the pull was getting stronger by the minute, I became more determined than ever to arrive at the top of that hill.

With barbed wire fencing to the left and right of the gate, I parked the car and carefully began to crawl through the fence to enter the property. On foot, I forged ahead, plowing through brush, overgrown Manzanita bushes and scrub Oak trees. Climbing the hill, I finally reached the summit where I could walk around in the clearing as if it was arranged for my arrival. With a massive plateau at the highest point, it appeared as if someone had already prepared a pad ready to be built upon. This pad was of natural formation, and the view was vast and stunning. Unbeknownst to me at the time, I was standing on top of a 71-acre parcel of land.

Dressed in slacks, long sleeves, and a tie, in Redding's Summer heat of 100 plus degrees, I walked around that gorgeous hilltop and prayed for over an hour. The presence of the Lord was tangible. I was filled with a mixture of both peace and growing anticipation. Being a visionary by nature, I could easily see the formation of a new church campus developed on this property. He is an incredible God. Previously, I had dismissed what I 'saw' in the Spirit as being just my natural man; however, not today. In order not to get ahead of my creative self, I continued to engage the Holy Spirit and allow Him to indelibly imprint upon my heart all I was experiencing.

The last half-hour of my prayer walk, I stumbled onto a dilapidated advertising sign that was lying face down. Lifting up this crumbling, weathered, and dirty sign so I could read it; there it was – the listing agent and a phone number. It had been for sale! I was genuinely excited and now even more-so, full of holy determination. When I left my car, I didn't think to bring a pen or paper, so I was unprepared to write anything down. This was, of course, the pre-cellular phone era, so I purposefully repeated the number over and over again in my mind until I had it memorized.

Quickly, I headed back down the small path I had forged to seek out a pay phone. The nearest phone at that time was approximately 3 miles away on the corner of Churn Creek and Dana Drive. There was no direct access off of Churn Creek Drive like there is today. The road dead-ended right where Fire Station 8 now resides. However, upon reaching the pay phone, which no longer exists, I hurriedly called the number on the sign. To my surprise, the realtor answered directly. I began asking questions about the property, and her bewildered responses caught my attention. Yes, she was the listing agent; but it had been a very long time since anyone had called on the listing, much less shown any interest in this piece of land. She was taken aback by my "sudden" attraction to it. This beautiful and most strategic property was magically positioned at the major crossroads of the city of Redding, which had a population of only 50,000 at the time.

Hurrying back to my office, I began to write down the things I'd heard the Father speak to me: the property's access, available acreage, growth potential — and even better yet — strategic alignment for visibility and taking dominion. Little did I know, He had already set the stage, raised the curtain, and the cast was about to enter.

I called a meeting with the church leadership team, and the brilliance of God's plan began to evolve. He is a deliberate and specific God. How deliberate? That property was listed for hundreds of thousands more than we eventually paid for it. Believing that the land we now wanted had been kept secret for such a time as this, we devised a fascinating offer to buy the

God is deliberate and specific, He misses nothing!

property with the terms in our favor: a $100,000 down payment, along with periodic payments until it was paid in full. There was no set payment schedule. It was basically "pay-as-you-can." The only stipulation was that we could not make any improvements on the property until the land was paid in full. This creative financing permitted us the opportunity to draw blueprints for the upcoming building and surrounding structures while successfully phase in each dimension physically, spiritually, and financially.

The property owners lived many states away receiving few and irregular updates on the property, much less inquiries or offers to purchase. To our astonishment, they accepted the offer with almost reckless enthusiasm. Up to this time and in such an exclusive area, I had never before experienced a real estate transaction that progressed so quickly and under such favorable terms. It was the beginning of a *Shift* that would change our lives and our church forever.

I ascertained later that the Realtor's sign had fallen down long before my discovery of the property and of course no one thought to check on the visibility of that advertisement. Apparently, the owners had either lost hope for a sale or became distracted and perhaps disinterested from the need to sell it at all. It was as if the Father had kept it hidden and set aside for us and for the right time and purpose. Further on in this book, I will reaffirm and support with scripture how that last statement is very true. It was a deliberate plan kept for us by the Father.

The Father keeps things hidden and set aside for you for the right time and purpose.

The unveiling of this property was the first recognizable heavenly *Shift* over our leadership team and Bethel Church, in Redding,

California. The House of God was growing. You could sense something different was taking place, both in leadership and in the congregation. From our Sunday services to our prayer meetings, we received affirmation and confirmation from the heart of God that we were heading in His chosen direction, and that a unique Spiritual transition was beginning.

People often talk about the changing of seasons, and it did feel somewhat like that. However, this was a season that would not end. It was to become a permanent change in spiritual alignment over the House of God and over our city. We did not know what this change would be, nor did we plan to measure it. We merely heard what the Father said and did it with obedience — hearing and doing, just as Jesus did.

The overflow of obedience manifested in unity and breakthroughs that came quickly and far more easily. Although progress seemed, incrementally small and inconsistent, we moved forward in a most distinctive measure. Truly, the unlimited Favor of the Most High seemed to rest over us personally and corporately. **A heavenly SHIFT was taking place.** The Father was preparing us for so much more!

A HEART PREPARATION FOR ACCELERATION

It was months later, and Bethel Church was flourishing greater than we thought was possible. So many changes were occurring, yet the outflow of the Holy Spirit remained constant. Signs and miracles were a daily event. The Spirit of the Lord flowed freely in our services. We saw unimaginable growth and an increase in vibrancy from those who attended regularly. Faith was rising, and people interacted and engaged as a unified church body. Relationships were forming with one another and within the community. When this begins to occur in you, it becomes evident around you. It was working. We were building an authentic reputation of compassionate capitalism in our city as the presence of the Lord was becoming tangibly visible to those living in and amongst the region. It was great to see a community evolving within our congregation, as bonds of trust were growing stronger. I look back on those days with a thankful heart and a sense of humility that He chose me for that season of vision casting, building and laying the foundation for the then-future we know as today.

Bethel Church had progressed rapidly in just a few short years since I first took the helm of leadership in 1984. Yet as it grew, we still lacked the financial ability to complete the purchase of the 71-acre parcel God had so miraculously provided for us. Our budget did not have one additional penny to build the desperately needed, new facility. In spite of the blessings, we had persistent challenges. I cannot recall a day, since the beginning, that was not filled with conflict and tension. You know that constant, 'push-against-all-that-you-believe-and-live' pressure? That's the one. Yes, we were advancing, but not without consistent opposition that stared on day one.

When the SHIFT occurs in you, it becomes evident around you.

AN UNPLANNED EXIT

It was astounding how I became Senior Pastor. I was elected January 15, 1984, and first stood in the pulpit March 4th of that year (See Gallery of Photos). I was 29 years of age and quite young for such advanced responsibilities. Apparently, the Father knew I was cut out for the task at hand. My late wife and I left a very large and flourishing singles group we had grown at Capital Christian Center in Sacramento, California, to accept the position in Redding.

It's humorous how the strategic plans of the Father are woven into our lives often when we aren't looking for them. For example, I gave no forethought to a simple statement back in 1980, when on vacation near Redding with my family. We visited Whiskeytown Reservoir on the fourth of July weekend. To participate in the celebration, we drove up to the Shasta Dam where, during that year, the City of Redding displayed their fireworks show, in which thousands gathered to watch. I saw hundreds of teenagers and young adults join in the holiday celebration in unruly behavior mixed with alcohol, drugs or both. Moved in my heart, I casually prayed, "God, if you love this City, you will send someone here to reach it." Little did I know I was speaking prophetically over His very intentions. The Father not only heard me, but He also infused me with the compassion to walk it out. Four years later he plucked me up and out of a thriving place of success, as man would see it, and planted me into that very city.

"God, if you love this city, you will send someone to reach it."

Upon arriving, I assumed leadership of a very troubled group of about 50 attendees which quickly reduced to 30! This small gathering survived four previous Senior Pastors along with a several church splits. On top of that, I inherited a staff that were emotionally and spiritually injured by those who had led before me. At times their behavior was quite distrusting of a new, young pastor. This was not my idea of an easy road especially after building such a strong, dedicated group at Capital Christian Center.

A humorous anecdote to the condition of things, I remember the first memorial service I ever performed. It was only a few weeks after arriving in Redding. I was carelessly speeding down Cypress Avenue, driving in a hurry to get to Lawncrest Memorial Chapel where I was officiating for a funeral. Looking up, I noticed the red flashing lights in my rear-view mirror. I pulled over to the side of the road waiting for my much-deserved ticket. Yes, I was speeding and caught the attention of a dutiful Redding Police officer. As he was writing the ticket, we started talking. He eventually got around to asking me how I earned a living in Redding. I told him I was a new pastor in town and obviously late for a funeral. Pressing in further he then inquired, "What church?" I quickly blurted out, "Bethel Church" to which He looked at me in shocked astonishment. Pausing for a moment, he then tore up the ticket, turned and said, "You have enough problems. Slow down and have a nice day." I can laugh today, but back then I was aghast and flabbergasted at his response! What had I gotten myself into?

COURAGE AND CHARACTER

The first two years of pastoring I was busy dealing with what seemed to be continuous unresolved people-problems. As a young, eager leader with a big heart for people, I didn't turn anyone away. With a "no defeat" attitude, I took on challenges that perhaps today, I would most likely refer out to more experienced professionals.

During one appointment in my office, I was scheduled to counsel a married woman who attended our church. Responsibly, I had a female attendant present to provide a more comfortable and safe environment for her and myself. When she arrived at my office, I took notice of her demeanor. She appeared beaten down, discouraged, and fearful. She began sharing situations and interactions with her spouse that concerned me, so I offered to meet with them both and rescheduled the new appointment immediately.

At their next appointment and within the course of their communication, a violent interaction surfaced between them. It was apparent that this behavior was common within their marriage. During that visit to my office, her husband became irate and physically aggressive, so I dismissed him. They remained as part of the church attending less and less until eventually, she divorced him. He must have decided in a moment of delusion that I somehow played a role in her independent decision to leave him. Since he believed the divorce was my fault, he decided to make a public statement about it. I mean a public statement with action.

This man stood across the street, in front of the Bethel church parking lot, which then resided at 2150 N. Bechelli Lane, and picketed me personally, before and after each service of the three services held every Sunday morning. He remained faithful to his mission and defamation of character for seven long years! His signs depicted accusations about me that were simply untrue. However, due to our constitutional rights of free speech, legally he was allowed to remain. Imagine trying to lead, much less grow, a church with this routine insult present in your face three times every Sunday for seven years. This guy's anger made way for bitterness to take root in his heart, which then played out in this bizarre behavior. Yet, the Lord required that I walk this out with humility, maintaining a forgiving heart. Little did I know it was an essential, external pressure He intended for my internal character formation. Deliberate growth that brought forth a greater promotion many years later. The Father strategically designs a foundation for our

External pressure is intended for internal character formation.

spiritual journey. Each challenge you face lays a stone on the path that leads to the fullness of the Father's intended design for you.

All along our church was flourishing, and we were able to pay for the parcel of land up on the hill, despite the unusual events mentioned above. I can now see the design He had for me not only prepared my heart for promotion, but He also prepared for my success against another spiritual assault I was about to confront. The enemy will always attack the best of what God has planned for you. One of satan's characteristics is jealousy, and specifically, envy of the Glory deserved and reserved for the Father.

THE PRESSURE COOKER CONTINUES

A series of events brought more heat to the already intense duress that our small team was already experiencing. Before acquiring the 71 acres on the hill, I had already heard from the Lord that we were to sell our current facility. So, I began looking for a buyer. Although we moved forward collectively with this decision, this too stirred up opinions and rumblings amongst the leadership. Our church on 2150 N. Bechelli Drive had been on the real estate market for approximately two years now. The rational thought was to sell the current facility, and then rent back from the new owner on a month-to-month basis until we built the new complex. This strategy would then give us time to acquire additional finances to begin building on the new site.

Finally, after a long time on the real estate market, an offer came to present to the church board. Negotiations were in place and after weeks of consideration, advisement, and frequent board meetings, we rejected the proposal with great disappointment. Had we accepted this offer, it would have literally cost the church a great deal more money at the completion of the sale and rent-back term of the lease. Suddenly, immense tension compounded when the rejected offer from the real estate investor turned into a lawsuit. This was no small lawsuit. Should the investor successfully obtain a favorable judgment, it could bankrupt the church. He demanded we perform on the offer, or he was filing a lawsuit against us. His basis, a point-of-order for the rules of a Non-profit corporation, didn't even involve the offer. He was meddling in the business of the church.

This action halted all forward movement towards the goals of building a new facility almost instantly. Water was poured upon our blazing fire of passion; nonetheless, we were determined to stay the course. Talk about feeling immobilized in a nanosecond! I was unaware of just how much Shift was genuinely occurring, both in me and in this situation. The pressure we felt was a spiritual dynamic that apparently was essential to what God had in store. He had to forge our hearts to handle a greater outpouring of His presence, and bring a significant realignment for the awakening of a city.

God has to forge our hearts to handle a greater outpouring of His presence.

For us, this involved a public, four-year, drawn-out and expensive legal process. It seemed like we were trapped. All the while supernatural changes were occurring that would deliver victory and launch an astounding season of blessing and influence for our local body. It was then that a series of events began shaping my belief in Solomon's proverb — "The wealth of the sinner is laid up for the righteous." This would forever now be clarified and refined within me.[1]

REVELATION IN THE FOURTH WATCH

One night I went to bed heavy-hearted, feeling weighted down over this legal problem and the effect it would have upon us. I was battling with anger and frustration as I felt trapped in a conflict we did not deserve. I could be the first pastor to lose an entire church and its building in a court case; one that should not be happening. During the fourth night of the watch, which is the last quarter of time before dawn, I was awakened with a phenomenal revelation from the Father. He clearly showed me what stance and attitude I must exemplify during this legal onslaught.

Immediately upon arousal, the Father spoke to me about a specific story in Isaiah, Chapter 36. This story was about King Hezekiah and the attempted siege of Jerusalem by King Sennacherib and his Assyrian army. The Assyrians had already cut off all supplies from moving in and out of the city. No water or food was available. Then the Assyrian messenger and intimidating army surrounded Jerusalem with fortified camps layered with rows of weapons and entrapment manned with archers, and warriors ready to advance with a mere word from the General leading the assault. It appeared like there was no way out and utter defeat was imminent. There was no reason for such aggression except a power play of position and authority. You see, King Hezekiah reformed the priesthood. He decreed there would be no other gods; thus he purged the idols from within the city. He took down the Assyrian high places, and in doing such, he did not make any agreements with, nor rely upon, Egypt for his provision. Instead, King Hezekiah relied on God and prayed for deliverance at His hand only.

Then right at the point where Sennacherib's army would take siege, the Lord declares to King Hezekiah, "I will deliver you." And so, it was. Instantly, in one day, the Lord delivered the Kingdom of Judah. The enemy's plan had been completely reversed. The fulfillment of prophetic words which were spoken was exactly as the Lord declared it would be. Suddenly, Israel was delivered not just from a complete takeover, but their lives were fully restored, and provision began to flow again out of what seemed to be an impossible situation. I was about to experience the same remarkable *Shift* in a legal 'siege' as Hezekiah did in a physical one.

My heart was torn with emotions from the continual conflict I faced almost everywhere I turned. I began feeling like this may never come to an end. All I could do was hold onto His words of promise. Days turned into months with no change in sight. Nevertheless, during that

> **Sometimes, all we can do is hold onto His words of Promise.**

time, the Lord continued to confirm His promises to me. On one unforgettable night, God spoke three specific things that I was to follow in the coming season of increase.

First, He counseled me regarding the condition of my heart. As breakthrough and victory came, it would be necessary that His character be evident in my choice of words and actions; nothing more and nothing less. God then led me to II Chronicles, Chapter 20. Here King Jehoshaphat was being invaded by the Moabites, the Ammonites, and others. The Lord spoke to King Jehoshaphat in verse 15 that the battle is not the people's, but God's. One of my favorite quotes is in Chapter 20, verse 17, "You will not have to fight this battle. Take up your position, stand firm and see the deliverance the Lord will give you, Judah and Jerusalem. Do not be afraid; do not be discouraged. Go out to face them tomorrow, and the Lord will be with you" (NIV).

Bowing his face before the Lord, King Jehoshaphat and the people worshipped the Most High God. The next day, King Jehoshaphat did just that; nothing more and nothing less. He instructed worshippers to go before the army shouting praise right into battle, and the rest is history. To receive that answer in the heat of an apparent defeat would cause anyone to drop and bow. However, the heart of worship comes out of a King who is in relationship to the Father.

Fill your heart with praise and thanksgiving and bless your enemies.

The second directive the Holy Spirit said was, "Fill your heart with praise and thanksgiving and stand to see the salvation of the Lord." I was to do nothing on my own in attempting to bring a solution to this problem. Moreover, the Lord counseled me how to answer the critics, both within and without, who always question why things happen. He instructed me to hold my tongue on all negative matters while this legal battle ensued.

Third and finally, He advised me to speak blessing over my adversary. This was something I had never fully grasped until my friend, John Dawson, wrote the book Taking your Cities for God.[2] Reading that book gave me a window and frame of reference to which I could say to myself, "Ah, that is how this works." The Holy Spirit said we would release a greater *Shift* by keeping a joyful spirit and a thankful heart. I was told to keep my focus on why He brought me here, and to remember Zechariah 4:6b; "It's not by might, nor by power, but by my Spirit," says the Lord.

HISTORY RECORDS THE GLORY

The Father often allows your adversary to do things that others think will bring them a greater advantage. Yet in the long run, it's just positioning your enemy for defeat. On our first day in court, we began jury selection. In a swift move, our opponents' counsel dismissed the jury and decided to have a trial wherewith the outcome would be decided exclusively by a Judge. Our legal counsel was caught off guard and was not remotely excited about taking our case to a Judge. He wanted a jury of local citizens to fully hear the case. At the time, it appeared to be a brilliant legal maneuver by our opponent, but in the end, it proved to be a terrible decision for him. His request became a key component bringing the victory our Lord delivered to us. Why would an experienced local real-estate attorney make such a move? I did not understand then; however, I see it now. It was as if the Lord whispered instructions into the ear of our opponent's attorney, planting ideas which carried the victory for us.

The now four-year-old lawsuit finally went to court. We were embroiled in accusation and attack. It was not looking favorable for us, at least in the mind of this thirty-something-year-old pastor. There were days I was so very discouraged. All I was able to do was to rehearse the directives the Father had given me about this assault and recall how I was to respond to each situation. I was to praise God for victory, like the choir on Jerusalem's wall in II Chronicles, Chapter 20. I was not to respond to any accusations, all the while speaking blessing over our accuser.

From my seat in the back of the courtroom, I was positioned to watch the beginning manifestations of a literal *Shift* in the heavenlies, right here on earth. For the earth is the Lord's and the fullness thereof! The next few days and months would astoundingly prove the promise in Proverbs 13:22b, "The wealth of the sinner is laid up for

> **"The wealth of the sinner is laid up for the righteous."**
>
> Proverbs 13:22b

the righteous." A first glimpse of this promise would be carried out in a courtroom of man's law.

Presenting the case to the judge lasted an entire week. On the last day, I sensed another *Shift* in the heavenlies before I left the courtroom. No, there was no victory. In fact, no decision had been made at all. What transpired the final day in court was so revealing and so matter-of-fact, it literally caused my mouth to drop open. After all the testimony was taken, and each lawyer had presented their closing statements, the judge sat quietly for a moment. It was more than a pregnant pause. Those few minutes felt like an eternity, and it seemed like there was no hope for this situation. When the judge spoke, he asked our attorney if he had anything further to add for consideration before he adjourned.

It was then the Holy Spirit whispered to me to request that our opponent, and accuser, who brought the lawsuit against us, be cross-examined again. Upon calling him back to the stand and still under oath, our attorney engaged him in conversation about previous business ventures he was involved in, unrelated to this hearing. Obviously, our opponent thought the case was concluded. In casual discussion with our legal counsel, words flowed out of his mouth that exposed the real nature of his attack on me and the church. Truth always prevails! His real intentions were to take the property from our church, using legalities unrelated to a purchase. He never intended on purchasing the property, just laid a trap to snag the property with legalese. He boasted of his previous court cases that concluded in his favor; similar non-profit organizations that lost properties due to nonprofit process. He gloated over their inexperience that became his legal victory. Through his answers, the motives of his heart were clearly defined. I was astounded. This was apparently beyond mere human strategy. We had not yet been officially exonerated, but we were already vindicated where it mattered most: heaven's courtroom. It would soon become evident in the physical dimension as well. It was just as God spoke to me, "Stand and see the salvation of the Lord!" The court was adjourned, and soon after we received a victorious judgment in our favor!

At this point, the journey was laden with defeat and a looming financial disaster. With just one word from the Lord, and the entire situation "**Shifted**." Defeat and injustice came to a screeching halt, and the influx of His favor and prosperity burst forth like a mighty river. The pressure now released, my heart was overjoyed as described in Proverbs 13:12b, "But a longing fulfilled is a tree of life." That to me became an understatement! Little did I know that He would deliver us almost instantaneously, without the manipulating hand of man and in a way that everyone would see that victory was from the Lord. This triumph was followed with an unanticipated financial release. The storehouse was open, and the abundant *Shift* was taking place.

Of course, looking back, I see it clearly! We were in the School of Supernatural Warfare. The Spirit's training was not just for one battle, one season, nor one reason. It was training for a permanent *Shift* that would continue beyond this event, even beyond future challenges bringing a dynamic mentality I call, 'Spiritual Occupation' under an open heaven for our city.

Psalm 144, verse 1 reads, "Praise be to the Rock, who trains my hands for war and my fingers for battle." It is also declared in II Corinthians, Chapter 10, verse 4, "For the weapons of our warfare are not carnal, but mighty through God to the pulling down of strongholds." The Father wants strongholds torn down, and torn down permanently. This victory was the beginning of the a personal *Shift* in my heart and one I walked out through my actions — the permanent *Shift* is an unending, open heaven. One more stepping stone laid for the individual and generational purposes of God.

Soon, greater abundance in all areas of life began to occur and continued growing until it birthed a greater spiritual influence over our entire city. It all happened in just a few months—and— just as the Lord said it would! Every battle we encountered, we won. The Father kept His word, "Victory in a day," and He even brought the spoils of the enemy to us. The Heavens have remained open, and all those who walked that journey participated in the victory! Bethel Church in Redding, California has continued to build upon the foundations we laid before them. The current leadership, who succeeded my tenure, have taken the influence that was given over the church and the city and spread it to many nations all for God's glory.

That being said, the *Shift* happened in the natural and in the spiritual in 1991, as we watched with our own eyes. That was when the Lord strategically aligned everything, even man, to reveal the truth of His 'wealth' and 'influence' that the Lord purposed and destined for us. Spiritual prosperity began then, and continues to this day as the favor of the Lord is upon that house—His house. It is now our privilege and responsibility to sustain the spiritual *Shift* the Father started.

A KEY IN VICTORIES TO COME: REMEMBER!

Our culture can be so busy with the 'now' and the 'next,' that we forget the true origins of breakthrough and miss how to sustain it; *a sign of true Spiritual Prosperity*. Jewish perspective is about the written and oral history of God's supernatural acts that took them from slavery to inheritance. Thus, the Torah, including the oral traditions found in the Midrash, is required learning for every Hebrew from generations back and to this day.

Israel began to fall when it failed to remember the things God had accomplished. Without a heart of appreciation and continual remembrance, you will forget and depend on other things rather than God; His ways, His patterns, and His future blessing. Likewise, in our culture, we must remind every generation what God started, the details of the journey, the process and how He brought the Victory!

Bethel Church went from crisis to astronomical blessing and then expanded the existing complex reaching international recognition. Remembering history is essential to sustain what the Father intends to continue. He desires that we live from glory to glory, so generations can look back to historical markers, just like Israel does.

These markers are not insignificant, but the original pivot points of a heavenly *Shift*, and the subsequent release that has produced growth now for 20+ years and counting. When living in current prosperity these principals can be ignored or forgotten, but honor begins here as man's heart remains in awe of God.

A change of leadership and the pains of transition has nearly erased these essential building blocks of **HIS story** — which is forever imprinted upon my journey and my heart. This is the truth our Father wants to be remembered and memorialized, for His glory to demonstrate honor, place value, and build a legacy of what He has done from the beginning. Just like Abraham, His blessings apply to us today! When we learn to regard all the ways of God, we can bring transformation, be it in a church, a city, or a culture. Remembering grows faith. It anchors your heart and keeps you steadfast in whatever journey He has called you to. This will empower you to finish the task in difficult times and reap His reward.

THE STOREHOUSE RELEASED

Our courtroom victory and the astonishing blessings that followed were not just a single, nor a series of events. They were a permanent spiritual change caused by the Lord. A God-breathed *Shift* which remains over that house to this day.

Are you ready for a *SHIFT* that places you into spiritual prosperity?

Are you ready for a *Shift* that opens the storehouse of God and catapults spiritual prosperity? This is far better than a mere financial increase. Experiencing His *Shift* over, in, and through you so much so that it overflows into your daily life, where changes come naturally and easily. A heart that longs for relationship with the Father, in the center of all you do and where you go, will transform you! Then it will flow over to people and families around you. It will intoxicate the corporate church, the cities they live in, and the nations we bring it to! He is an all-inclusive God and has all you need available for whoever chooses to participate. It's all up to you.

You see, the 'wealth' of the sinner is laid up for the 'righteous' as Proverbs 13:22b states. King David built the treasury, and his son, King Solomon lived the transfer and personally understood it. He fully expected subsequent generations to experience it at much greater levels. Jesus came to fulfill the law and the prophets. To change the culture, a generation must walk in the heartbeat that Jesus Himself modeled. With an open heaven, Jesus understood life, influence, prosperity, and transformation greater than King Solomon. He said in John 14:12, ". . . Whoever believes in Me will also do the works that I am doing. He will do even greater than these . . ." Believing causes us to live under heaven's economy and culture. We will live a life full of wisdom that emanates through us bringing dramatic spiritual and cultural change.

I was privileged and honored to participate in the Father's plan laying the foundation during my years as Senior Pastor of Bethel Church. I experienced an open heaven personally and received a glimpse of what God intends to bring to our generation. Today's release is a much greater measure. Seeing His storehouse accessed and used by the body of Christ is my passion. It is also my heart's desire to share it with you! As an old radio personality used to say, "Now it's time for the rest of His story." I pray according to Ephesians 1:15ff "that the Father may illuminate the eyes of our hearts that we may see." **The Shift has begun**. The transfer of wealth and influence from His storehouse to your house is unstoppable if you follow His heart, learn His ways, and take direction only from Him.

CHAPTER TWO

THE LORD BREAKS OUT BEFORE ME

THE ADVENTURE GROWS

A few weeks following the final week in court, we received notice that the plaintiff had lost the lawsuit. Immediately, our legal counsel advised me to countersue for court costs and damages. Wow, what a thought. Who wouldn't want to recover all that money spent, much less the time wasted on wrongful accusation and selfish motive? I had been so consumed with the legal battle, that I could not pursue the things we really needed to apply our energy and efforts to. Namely, we needed to secure a loan to facilitate building the complex on the 71-acre parcel we had acquired in such a miraculous fashion.

God does not judge time and resources, as we do from our finite view. So, my first thought about recovery was, "YES, now that is justice!" Later that night, however, God graced me with another 'Aha' moment where I was admonished to forgive that individual and pursue no further legal entanglements, specifically, no retaliation and no countersuits.

Bringing our legal options before the leaders of the church, provided me an opportunity to share what God had disclosed to me earlier. It was a moment when, as the Father's representative, you merely state the directive of the Lord, and it will be so. A key lesson here is obedience. The Lord honors those who obey even when conventional wisdom says to pursue another path. Although the church leadership was not in complete agreement, I held my ground and did exactly as the Lord instructed, which brought everyone peace. During those four, long years I had plenty of time for the attitudes of my heart to become more like the His. Remember God had counseled me about that early on in the battle. Naturally, His character was now more evident, even to me. However, this time the Father required even more. By example, I was to lead the church and the leadership team into forgiveness over the whole legal incident. We were to forgive, bless and love; not retaliate. This was a pivotal spiritual moment that would change the course of our Fellowship and my life forever.

One cannot afford to miss those 'Aha' or course-correcting moments. As we try to navigate and fulfill the will of God, He is always faithful to speak in a way we can receive and act upon it.

In II Samuel, Chapters 5 through 10, the Lord had established David as King. David brought the Israelites through many victorious battles. With the recovery of the Ark of the Covenant, the King danced and worshipped before the Lord. He knew great restoration was coming and God was bringing to the Israelites the joy of fulfillment. God's Kingdom was expanding, and he had afforded David and the people a time of rest, while peace was becoming prevalent in the land.

In Chapter 7, David, like many of us, with all enthusiasm and passion, decided he wanted to honor God. There he is living in a palace, "A house of Cedar" as he puts it, and "The Ark of the

Covenant is sitting in a tent." David decides then and there, he was going to build a temple to adequately house the presence of the Almighty. Nathan, his prophetic companion, responds to the King with, "Do whatever is in your heart to do." That evening, however, Nathan experienced an 'Aha' from God. Imagine that! God thwarted the kings plans to do something splendid for David. You see, God delights in doing for His people. It brings Him great pleasure to fulfill His beloved's hearts' desire.

God spoke to Nathan and told Him very directly that He has been content in where His presence was housed. It is not about the attributes of location. It's surely not about the grandeur. However, it was all about God's command for obedience. This time, it was His agenda that becomes a reality. In summary, God instructs Nathan that David is to 'receive' all that He has established and provided for Him. This was not to be a season of doing. This was, in fact, a season of watching the powerful hand of the Lord fulfill all that He promised His people. God

The Lord brought David from the pasture to the palace to inhabit and enjoy all His provision.

Himself was going to establish David's throne. The Lord brought David from the pasture to the palace, and David was to inhabit the land and enjoy all the provision that was coming! Not only that, God would make David's name great and provide the people with a home where they would not be disturbed. Furthermore, Jehovah had reserved the privilege of building Himself a temple, which David's son would accomplish. Not only would the Father establish King David's throne, but even his son's throne forever! The Father was giving David the fruit of lineage. It was his son's assignment, and not to be stolen. God gave David a gentle, but very firm course correction II Samuel 7:10-17. (NIV).

In retrospect, as I look back now on the astonishing provision of the Lord, to countersue would have displaced the greater thing God was about to do! When He is on a mission to give, we must, as His children, learn how to receive. His magnificence is revealed greatly in deliverance, but more so in the abundance found in the gift of fulfillment. The Father is longing and waiting to unleash His blessings upon us. He is clearly more focused on releasing His favor and blessing over us, than what we can do for Him.

A STRANGE PHONE CALL

By nature, I am a networker, and so I made that a priority in our city. When my secretary informed me that someone unfamiliar to me had requested an appointment, I was intrigued but waited patiently for the meeting. My office was then located at the previous church site on N. Bechelli Drive. It was a beautiful location with incredible views. The church building had been built up on the bluffs overlooking the Sacramento River. It was a strip of land that was extremely valuable, and to my surprise, much sought after.

The day of the scheduled appointment finally came. When the mystery man arrived at my office. He introduced himself as Lee Salter, the attorney for Leah McConnell, co-founder of the McConnell Foundation; a non-religious charitable foundation. Leah McConnell sent Lee with a mission and a message. She wanted to buy our 5-acre complex. This seemed too good to be true. Although I had, from time to time, heard of the McConnell Foundation, and their charitable foundation, I had never crossed paths with them personally. After many unsuccessful attempts to sell our church property, and then the lawsuit that kept it unsalable for four years, this astonishing offer was quite unexpected and felt as if it came out of nowhere.

The price we needed to move forward was represented directly in this offer, and may I add, without any effort on our part. There was no professional real estate agent involved, and furthermore, not one negotiation occurred! The price was exactly right, and the timing could not have been better. The only glitch was that our church body did not possess the resources yet to build another complex. Especially one with the magnitude we thought the Lord was showing us to build. Large commercial lending for churches was very hard to come by, much like it is today. Those thoughts and more raced through my mind. "So, what do you do now?" I rambled through my head, "Sell this facility and have to lease back what you once owned, yet unable to build the new complex?" I thanked Mr. Salter for their generous offer, and let him know I would respond in an adequate measure of time.

Humbled at the startling supply that just landed before me, I was grateful, but continued to ponder on the financial future at the same time. I should have been dancing on the tables and celebrating how it was coming together, but like all of life's journeys, walking out the details can excite and entangle us at the same time. After waiting before the Lord, I scheduled a board meeting. Together, our leadership met for prayer and reviewed the generous offer. With all the Lord had done, surely, He had no intentions of stopping now. Again, He said to me, "Stand and see the Glory of the Lord." It was the next right step to take.

"Stand and see the Glory of the Lord."

THE FATHER'S LAUGHTER

Psalms 2:4a reads, "The one enthroned in heaven laughs." God does have a sense of humor, and I suspect He finds humor in many things we may not think are quite so funny. The twist to this story must have come from the Father's sense of humor, in that the choices of man are well within the plans of God. It seems that the Lord orchestrates so much more in our lives than we credit Him with, perhaps more times than not. It has repeatedly crossed my mind how He enjoys working in and through our situations. At least I believe this opportunity must have employed all of heaven in laughter. "A man makes his plans, but the Lord determines his steps," as it clearly reads in Proverbs 16:9. So many times we become immersed in the strategies of men, setting up an expected outcome, but the Father is sovereign. His capable hands orchestrated an extraordinary breakthrough. WOW!

In a comparably small city, the news always traveled fast. So why not now? Before our leadership could come to a consensus on this offer and determine any outcome, there was suddenly a new wrinkle. My office was in the back of the educational wing of our facility, which had all been converted into an office complex. Conveniently there was a back-parking lot with a private door to the complex. Upon entering, one would step down into the recessed space, and just to the left, you would find me conducting business.

One Wednesday morning as I was sitting at my desk working, I glanced through the window overlooking the parking lot and saw a very expensive convertible pull up. Someone stepped out of the car and made their way towards this back-entry door. Without a knock, the door opened, and a very well-dressed man stepped in. He was unannounced, uninvited and obviously on a mission. Speaking quickly, he introduced himself as Rod Rodriguez, a well-known social and financial figure in Redding. Next, he assertively stepped forward, dropped a legal sized envelope onto my desk and declared, "This is an offer to buy this property. As I participate on a number of nonprofit boards, I know the protocols to follow, and you must present this offer to your whole church membership for a vote; not to do so, can pose significant legal ramifications."

"Seriously?" I thought to myself, "Here we go again! Just out of one long, drawn-out legal battle and now here potentially is another one." Apparently, Mr. Rodriguez was not anticipating nor soliciting a response, as he just turned and walked out the same way he entered making no further comments upon his exit. I sat motionlessly and watched him get in his car and drive off. Stunned at what had just occurred I sat in silence. Immediately, I felt impressed by the Holy Spirit's voice, "Do NOT open this envelope, but seek me!" An outlandish peace then permeated the room. I walked over and fell on my office couch. Waiting there as directed, the Holy Spirit downloaded His detailed instructions on how to handle the entire situation. God is so faithful. He is simply faithful.

I am and have always tried to be, a man of my word. It is a core value that has both blessed me and cost me greatly. It is so significant that I have had to, on occasion, honor things that I had said off-the-cuff. However, when your core values are truly 'core,' it doesn't take any effort to know what to do. Considering the facts, options, benefits, and consequences is essential before making decisions. Once a decision has been made, however, the only consideration left is how to follow through; nothing more, nothing less, and always directed by the Lord.

When your core values are truly 'core,' it doesn't take any effort to know what to do.

Keeping my word was so deeply embedded in my heart, I had no other option regarding this new offer. I had already given my word to Leah McConnell, who generously offered to purchase our property. So, no matter what the risk or the consequences that may follow, my word must be fully kept to the McConnell Foundation. In alignment with the Word of God, and with the counsel of elders and attorneys, we followed a very deliberate and specific path the Lord had instructed as I had waited in obedience. Upon reviewing the second offer, so garishly delivered, it appeared to benefit the church with even greater revenue. Nevertheless, with the journey we had just completed and having seen the hand of the Lord in all He instructed me to do, the leadership supported the decision to hold fast to the first offer we received and accepted. That single moment was probably the most significant representation of a three-chord strand with leadership I have ever experienced throughout my entire time of service in that city. Little did I know, that the very virtue of God in me was being revealed to people I was totally unaware of. I was totally unaware. That is how character works. It's supposed to precede your going in, and leave the residue of your King when you vacate.

Character is supposed to precede your going in, and leave the residue of your King when you vacate.

THE WATER BREAKS FORTH

Like I said before, in small-town news travels fast and it proved to be true in this case. The second buyer, Mr. Rodriguez, had left determined, confident, and remained so. Mrs. McConnell remained silent and distant for days. Finally, a phone call came. Lee Salter was calling back on behalf of the McConnell Foundation. By now I was well aware that the heavens were opened and all things were coming into position. Watching with expectation, I was eager to see what the Father had planned next. With my ear finely tuned, my confidence and trust soaring at new heights, I recognized that He had been in my future preparing for my arrival.

During the conversation with Mr. Salter, this stately gentleman informed me that Mrs. McConnell wanted to upgrade her already-accepted offer and it would be delivered for my review. WOW! When the package came, I read and re-read the contents. The original offer had been adjusted. Mrs. McConnell not only wanted to reinforce that she wanted to buy the complex, but she increased the original purchase price by several hundred thousand dollars! Who does that?

Remember this was a contract that was already theirs! On top of that, the enclosed letter continued to share that this well-known Philanthropist was going to contribute a $500,000 donation to the new building project, but it wasn't over yet. There was more. There is always more when the Father says it is time to receive. God's hands were open, and His joy was being fulfilled as He began to pour out a bounty that shocked me to no end.

There is always more when the Father says it is time to receive.

Mr. Salter revised the offer then added a deal clincher. In addition to their increased purchase price to buy the 5 acres and their generous donation of $500,000, they extended to us the one thing that we could not seem to acquire. This independent foundation with no religious or spiritual affiliation proceeded with an offer to finance our entire commercial building project at an absolutely ridiculous, low-interest rate and allowed us to remain in our current facility on N. Bechelli Lane, **RENT FREE** until the new commercial building was completed. The words reverberated in my head, "Stand and see the Glory of the Lord" again. That's right, in one day Bethel Church went from conflict to abundance!

When I asked Mr. Salter why they not only changed their offer but made such an extravagant increase available to us, he said to me, "Mrs. Leah McConnell wanted to extend a 'Thank You' for keeping your word!" Sitting in amazement, with my heart full of thanksgiving and overwhelmed with joy at the faithfulness of the Father, I accepted the offer on behalf of our organization. The character of the Lord radiated from the heart of this leader, and He brought us an increase greater than we could have ever dreamed or imagined! I am humbled that the Father chose me to reveal Himself to this woman. Just like King David, I was to sit and 'receive' what the Lord had prepared for all of us in that moment. God's final tally of all that He delivered on that day, equaled millions of dollars in blessing and provision for the church. The reason we wrote this book is because the Lord spoke to Deborah late one night, telling her, "the **Transfer of Wealth** began when Leah McConnell saw the character of God in action."

He said this was the example He chose to represent the scripture: "The wealth of the sinner is laid up for the righteous." Better yet, the *Shift* is not coming, it's here and already in motion.

THE WEALTH OF INFLUENCE

Transformation as a goal has been buzzing around for a very long time. I have heard it spoken of, in and among many Christian groups. Ed Silvoso wrote a book about Transformation[1] that changes lives, families, cities, states, and nations. If you believe the Bible, then you believe it is possible to happen again; furthermore, it can happen now.

The Welsh Revival is one of those stories where transformation was nationwide and had an impact in every city. It all began with a man named Evan Roberts who began to preach. Soon the Spirit of the Lord fell, and revival reached every known community in Wales. There was such an out-flowing of God's presence drawing men unto Himself that taverns closed, jails were emptied, and violent men became lovers of God. Their whole culture was transformed and all without the strategies of man. When the Father determines He is going to move, He does so: on time, every time.

So, it was for us. The measure the Lord had given was an abounding overflow. As we moved forward with the building project, we remained in awe of His incredible love and bountiful blessing. Remember, every month we rented back at our own facility at no cost!

After experiencing so many financial miracles, we then noticed God's storehouse had been released into our house even encompassing areas of our personal and corporate life. Miracles

Miracles began to appear. Favor and influence were increasing.

began to appear in an accelerated fashion and ingenious ways. Favor and influence were increasing. God was clearly rising.

One unique miracle had to do with the city of Redding and the bureaucracy that typically accompanies government procedures. The building project was nearly completed; enough so that we had scheduled our first Sunday meeting at the new location. One Sunday night in early October 1993, we were concluding our final gathering at the N. Bechelli Lane facility. Our move-in date at the new complex was scheduled for the following Sunday. Thursday before moving in, the final inspection for our Certificate of Occupancy was scheduled. That particular day, I happened to be on site. As the city Building Inspector walked through our facility, he went through his list of items to issue us a pass or fail. Coming upon the requirements for the smoke dampers, he paused and began looking further into the installation as if something was wrong.

He then began to compare the actual work completed on our building with photos from an installation manual. He apparently determined the installation was not performed according to code. On the spot, with three days remaining before our first Sunday service, he canceled the issuance for our Certificate of Occupancy. We were stunned beyond words!

Boldly, unashamed and regardless of who was present, we began to pray for divine intervention. We did not call anyone but the Father, out loud, in prayer. All of a sudden, we heard screeching tires outside, and within minutes the front door of our facility burst open with immense energy. Prayer meeting immediately over, everyone looked to see what in the world was happening. In stepped the Fire Marshal arriving without notice and without invitation. It was as if an angel of the Lord had just rerouted the Marshall's course for the day and sent him directly to us to handle the situation. Nervously the building inspector sputtered why he had failed the final inspection and why he was not issuing us the necessary Certificate. Flying into a tirade, the Fire Marshall informed the Inspector that he did not understand fire code and that installation was completed precisely and according to local fire requirements. He then announced he would override the Inspector's determination and grant a 'Pass' on the final inspection. Once again, favor from above was extended to us. So much so, that even those in civil authority were inexplicably moved to act on our behalf.

THE INCREASE OF AN OPEN HEAVEN

Occupying our new building was such a pleasure. Not just because of the newness, but because we were experiencing the delight of the Lord. This new chapter in our church represented the Father's joy, moving provision from His storehouse to our house. It was personal and corporate. It was as though the floodgates of heaven were gushing wide-open over the entire 71 acres. The increase was evident; specifically, in watching so many new people coming to know Jesus Christ. The true manifestation of God's abundance and flow of His spirit is when you see the fruit of new growth. I'm not referring to church growth that comes when a family changes their attendance from one church building to another. No, I am happily speaking of those who may not have known Jesus Christ as Lord and Savior before, and now they do. That increase was breathtaking and the invasion of the Lord's presence, reaching segments of our city we had previously been unable to reach, was thrilling. Influence began to spread unlike anything I had seen in forty years of life. Local and State leaders were now networking with us, and without any solicitation or manipulation from our leadership (See article in Gallery of Photos).

The *Shift* of heaven was in full throttle. It began with us needing protection from man's law and continued with an avalanche of both financial and local blessings. Add to that, an insatiable hunger for the outflow of God's presence complete with Biblical signs, wonders, and miracles. I had an immense feeling of gratitude. Have you ever been overwhelmed by God? Completely taken aback both in mind and spirit with a sensation of the Father's delight in you? That is what God was doing for me personally, and to our church body. Unspeakable!

Drowning in appreciation, the Father spoke to me that this was just the beginning of His presence that should be normal and spread abroad. This was not to be an isolated pocket of His glory, but perpetual cascading waves that

We witnessed the greatest miracles of all—people finding Jesus!

would enter every door where He found His children starving for more of Him. Unusual miracles began appearing everywhere in and amongst people, whether or not they were connected to our Fellowship. We witnessed epic healings, extravagant provision, satanic works thwarted and the greatest miracle of all — people finding Jesus Christ. There was an open heaven over our network and spreading throughout the city. Heaven hovered over His house.

STONES LAID WITH PURPOSE

The phone rang and on the other end was the familiar voice of Jill Stacher. She was one of many personal intercessors and friends who journeyed with me when I served as Senior Pastor. She had just received an urgent call that a child under the age of two had drowned in their backyard pool. This family did not attend our church at the time. Jill was connected to a city-wide intercessory group and called me to help. Without any hesitation, I jumped into my car and sped over to the hospital where the baby lay lifeless. Because I was a Pastor, I was allowed into the examination room where the parents of the child were holding vigil at the bedside. After a few moments of prayer, we asked the nurses and other staff to leave us alone in the room. There she lay . . . lifeless.

Prompted by the Spirit, I did an unusual faith act. I laid my entire weight over the top of this little, motionless body, just as I had pictured what Elijah, the Old Testament prophet did. It was not an act of courage or desperation. I was not concerned about who was present, and I did not ask permission from the parents standing at the bedside. It was a natural, inert move propelled by the Spirit of God that lives in me. Out of response to His prompting, I merely obeyed. Although the baby did not live, I felt the Holy Spirit's confirmation that in the years to come, He would ask me to be ready to move without hesitation or consideration at whatever He prompted me to do. Today, Bethel Church is known worldwide for its courageous and passionate heart for healing the sick and dying. There are even reports of those who prayed in obedience, and the Father has brought life back into those who were lifeless. Obedience is always a stepping stone laid to walk further in the greater purposes of God.

Obedience is always a stepping stone laid to walk further in the greater purposes of God.

BACK TO THE FUTURE

As we write this book, I am reflecting on God's heart. The principles that positioned us to move forward are much clearer now more than ever. From 1991 through 1995, what belonged in the world's system as we know it, had *Shifted* to those who belonged to Jesus Christ, to be used for influence and authority. Although the wealth that was stored up and transferred to us was phenomenal; the manifestation of His delight poured out on us, the scripture fulfillment of His promise and desire was mind-boggling. Fulfillment after fulfillment, wave after wave, in regular increments exhibited the lavish love of the Father. This was just the beginning of what has now become a normal marker of the current surge in His presence. This season was about the Transfer, if you will. Authority and power had *Shifted*, tipping the scales in the spirit.

As Jesus walked on the earth, He lived with influence, power, and provision. This type of command is not typically seen in the spiritual circles as we've known them. Yet, this was a prevalent, daily occurrence during His life. He walked on the earth with a natural expectation to 'do life' in the same measure as if He were in heaven with His Father. When Jesus needed to pay taxes, He merely exercised His authority as was decreed in the Garden of Eden, and called the fish to bring the exact provision needed. Jesus' life was so ordinarily extraordinary that it confused those around Him. It messed with the natural elements of man's understanding here on earth. So, paradoxical to man's thinking was His lifestyle that when He moved as directed by His Father, it outraged the crowds and stirred up jealousies even in His hometown. They wanted to hurl him off a cliff. It didn't matter if Jesus walked on dirt or on the streets of gold, He functioned naturally with an influence distributed from the throne room of heaven.

Jesus' life was so ordinarily extraordinary that it confused those around Him.

FOR TODAY AND TOMORROW

Recently, the Father spoke to me and declared this kind of *Shift* will be spread throughout His bride. Wherever He finds hearts ready to receive, reveal and release in reckless abandon all that belongs to Him and will be given to fulfill His purposes. God is choosing those who will not share in His glory, nor relish in the authority He grants them. Most of all, the Father is looking for those who are willing to draw all men to Jesus Christ, His son. The growing vacuum in our culture will be filled with the fragrance of the Father's glory, and His power and presence will arise in available, chosen vessels. For some of you, this is a mere confirmation of what God has already spoken to you in secret. For others, it may be good news to your ears. For me, it is precisely where I intend to live. The place I want to be is where the Father is moving, not where He just left.

CHAPTER THREE

A MANDATE OF FULFILLMENT

HIS ORIGINAL INTENTIONS

Woven into the tapestry of man's journey is a unique, colorful strand that represents God's individualized intention for each of us. Then throughout our lives, when we see that familiar color, it will remind us that we are in the center of His will. Over the course of a lifetime, He remains relentless positioning opportunities for us, so that our highest dreams can be fulfilled. When we accomplish them, not only does the Kingdom of God enlarge, but we experience a deep satisfaction knowing we brought Jesus His reward.

When your divine purpose and natural accomplishments converge, it feels like a missile locked onto a target, and you can do nothing less than hit the bull's eye. You must grab hold of the realization that your *Shift* is here—now! The next step in God's master plan enables us to fulfill our assignment which was set before the foundation of the world. Let's review these markers.

In the beginning, the Father creates the heavens and the earth. He then creates man in His likeness and presents him with a mandate: "Go and take dominion over the earth." (Genesis 1:26-31 paraphrased). Arthur Burk, founder of Plumbline Ministries in Whittier, California calls this the "Garden Mandate."[1] Because of sin, man fell from grace which removed him out from under heaven's canopy of blessing. God's blessing, of course, included jurisdiction and authority. Thankfully, the Father in His resolute nature will always provide another opportunity where man can fulfill his eternal purpose and claim his birthright. Even during the darkest hours, when creation rebelled against the heart of our loving Father; He never hesitated in His pursuit of a never-ending relationship with those He dearly loves. Much like any natural father would pursue a lost or rebellious child, so will He, at any cost.

We catch the first glimpse of this when God reaches out to Noah, a righteous man, and preserves his seed. Then there is God's friendship with Abraham, where an unbreakable promise of love and blessing, was made between the two of them. God's bottomless love provided not only a lineage but even extended the blessing toward Abraham's children and children's children.

To cement God's pursuit of a genuine relationship with His people, He creates an operating agreement for them. A "covenant." This is the Law of Moses. This covenant known as the Torah, outlined in detail how man was to conduct their lives while engaging and accessing the Father. The new testament brought greater understanding as the new covenant gives us direct access to Him. The purpose, Old and New Testament, remains as a guideline for us today. Staying connected to and engaging the Spirit of the Lord is the basis for living as Jesus did. Functioning under an open heaven builds the momentum for exponential change. You see, the Law served a more-reaching purpose than simply setting the stage for the New Testament. God purposed that His covenant would not merely keep them out of bondage, but cause their hearts to yearn for and desire the relational covenant where Jesus expanded our freedoms in the New Testament. Made in His image, we all bear an inner witness that there has to be more.

In the beginning, Adam, Eve and the family knew what it was like to live and exist under all of heaven's power, blessing and increase. They were not estranged from anything in His spiritual domain. The Mosaic Covenant was an invitation for those He loved to reunite them in a measure all could engage Him, but at that time they did not choose it. Moses and his relationship with the Father personified the intimacy that the Father desires to have with each one of us; growing in friendship and encountering Him face to face. Now that's real relationship! King David also developed an extravagant intimate relationship with the Father, vividly outlined in Scripture. He walked with and pleased God in such an unprecedented measure that he was permitted to enter forbidden areas not yet available, according to the law and pre-dating Christ's restoration. How is this possible?

This intimacy displayed in the Word between God, and Noah, Abraham, Moses and David, was clearly not widespread. They were isolated pockets in history where the Father joyfully interacted with each of them, one on one. What made them different that God would choose them? Even David wondered out loud in 2 Samuel 7:18 and asks God, "Who am I Sovereign Lord, and what is my family that you have brought me this far?" I propose each one not only saw the invitation, but desired to engage Him and experienced the Father's heart poured out even more. The Lord answers David by telling him He will make his name great and even his children's name great. A legacy for this imperfect, dancing King was being designed and set up by the Almighty.

God's passion for a reunited intimacy with His creation now reaches a climax. He not only devised the plan, but He is vested.

> **The Father stays the course; faithful to finish what He starts.**
>
> Philippians 1:6

That means God has skin in the game! Here comes Jesus, the very Son of God, to legally cancel humanity's treason, completely pay the debt to satisfy and fulfill the law, and obliterate every barrier. Now, everyone can return to heaven's covering and engage with their Redeemer, the full Godhead, and return to their first position in the Garden. Jesus' resurrection not only closed the gap, but it paved a road for intimacy with every culture who wanted to be adopted into the expanded family God had just expanded. The Father stays the course, always faithful to finish whatever He starts; Philippians 1:6. Because of Jesus Christ, we now have the ability and legal right to function as mandated and in the fullness of His identity, be God's change agent here upon the earth.

The New Testament neither cancels nor contradicts the Old Testament. It is the epic story of Jesus fulfilling, or 'completing' the requirements of the Law, yet repositioning each of us to engage with our Father as He originally intended. All those that choose to follow Christ are allowed to participate in the plan started back in the Garden. The redemption of humanity brought the restoration of heaven's government back into our lives and thus back into our world. The earth, where we live, act, and occupy, is now to be under the jurisdiction of Christ living in and through redeemed people. Revelation 11:15 declares, *"The kingdoms of this world are now the kingdom of our Lord, and of His Christ, and he will reign forever and ever."*

HIS PLAN AN AERIAL VIEW

Western minds lean towards a compartmentalized, Greek understanding and application of the Bible rather than an integrated manner, as in the Jewish perspective, where it is a continuum. Like the Greek culture, we have categorized way too much and broken the Bible into independent, beneficial pieces. Often, we may receive partial understanding but frequently miss the larger picture. Whether it is taking a Scripture out of context, or merely searching for passages to fit our circumstances and defend our theology, we gravitate to this way of thinking.

As a young believer, I built my study of the Word based on smaller sections of reading, looking for the 'morsel' of truth. That, in and of itself, is neither wrong nor misdirected. However, seeing God's plan and all He has woven together as a single masterpiece, offers a new revelation of who you are and how He yearns for us to prosper. Today, I am studying the Bible with a new understanding and laser focused view. Why you may ask? So I can grasp the fullness of His heart, rather than a single component. When looking from an aerial perspective, you notice that light casts differently. This provides a much different and broader picture of the way God intentionally develops individual lives and people groups. His hand is working in and through the journey of all those He loves, for He is for us.

There are simple, yet profound elements that build a foundation for all of God's chosen people:

1. We were created for intimate relationship with God.

2. We are His chosen vessel to carry out His heart and His will on the earth and to prepare all things for the ages to come.

3. The Father is passionate about what happens on the earth He created, and desires for us to bring it under His complete operational authority as originally intended.

4. Redemption and restoration are paramount in the Father's purpose.

5. The by-product of Christ's redeeming blood produces transformed lives, families, cities, and eventually nations. Thus, completing His "Garden Mandate."

The Law of Moses was never intended to frustrate man over who God is or His motives toward us. Frustration only rises because the Old Testament covenant did not make full provision for us to fulfill our role completely. May I propose that it is written into our very DNA to rise up in the nature of God and take dominion in every area of life that we hold legitimate authority because of Jesus Christ? Our very nature aches to achieve, overcome and conquer. It is an inherent trait. So then, why didn't we?

Because until Christ bridged the gap that man created for himself, our wired-to-conquer-nature was in conflict with our limited abilities. We lacked legal access and opportunity to overcome. It's not hard for a Believer to discover that God's will can never be accomplished man's way. Not only is it not in our ability, but the Lord desires to work with us in relationship. Jesus ended the separation that sin created so together we can establish His purpose and complete restoration Heaven's way!

Heaven is God's throne and eternity's courtroom where all final decisions are made. So, when God speaks from His throne, it happens. His word does not return unto Him empty. Now we, who are in Christ under the covenant of grace, have no hindrances to accomplishing His wishes. By virtue of our adoption in Christ Jesus, we have the ability to accomplish whatever God says. His

Master Plan remains in effect and we are empowered and ready to fulfill it.

A CHANGE IN OPERATING SYSTEMS

When reading the New Testament from a Jewish perspective, and it comes into better focus. All the New Testament writers were Hebrew and understood that Jesus' new covenant was the next and concluding step. It would bring the completion of God's whole plan. The only Achilles heel was they lacked the vision to see the inclusion of Gentiles, non-Jewish people groups, fitting into the bigger picture.

True Hebraic thinking was and still is, all inclusive. This includes history, traditions, and customs that hold value—from the smallest of ideas to the greatest concerns of the future. So, when one reads the Bible from a western or Grecian mindset, we may often see it from an opposing point of view.

It's very similar to the way genders think and communicate, often so differently. When a man does not see where something fits, he packs it away without any need for an explanation and moves happily toward his next task at hand. Thus, they create individual 'rooms' that often don't connect. Traditionally, women consider the whole enchilada. She needs to feel the 'what' of yesterday, the 'why' for today, and the 'how' for tomorrow? It is an all-inclusive process of communication. Understanding the female way of communication can greatly assist you with the Hebrew thought process; it too, is all-inclusive. Why do you suppose satan has worked so hard to wipe out the Jewish bloodline, or in some cases made serious inroads to distance the modern Western church from Israel? The adversary's goal in banishing the Hebrew culture is not just to annihilate God's chosen bloodline, but to wipe out historical perspective and alliance for the Gentiles as well. The Scriptures declare in Ephesians 2:11-15, that both the Jewish people, along with grafted in Gentiles, will unify in Christ Jesus as "one new man" and complete the race set before them.

The New Testament writers spent a good amount of time addressing how 'thinking' turns into 'doing.' Most people understand that beliefs will result in action. For example, once during a counseling session, the married couple before me was battling a major disconnect in communicating with each other. Week after week they returned home with no real solution. Then it dawned on me. Each spouse was functioning within their marriage from opposite beliefs and viewpoints. His view of marriage and how to relate to his wife was in-the-moment, and problem-driven. He could not measure the moment against the backdrop of a whole lifetime. Her perspective was from the larger picture of an entire lifetime together, and so she felt it pointless to give all her energy to any single problem currently in front of them.

Like the husband in this example, the Church has approached our Lord and Kingdom life from an opposite perspective, beginning with man as the focal point. Therefore, Western mindsets interpret Scripture from an egocentric posture, "How does this apply to or benefit me?" That mindset compartmentalizes the 'God experience' and His influence or participation outside our day-to-day choosing. We meet God on the day of rest, which He asked us to observe and connect on. The New Testament authors, being Hebrew, naturally function with a Jewish operating system. God is their focal point. As they penned the Scriptures, they inscribed their message from an understanding that they are God's chosen people and all parts of their life integrate around Him as the center. Therefore, their choices affect God, His blessings, and His promises. The outcome of such choices will determine the value or quality of their life. All things affect all places in their world! This is an all-together different frame of reference; beginning with God (YHVH) in the midst of every part of their world. As you can see, each approach will yield a different understanding of Scripture. It's important that we obtain the Father's perspective immersed in the Hebrew culture, as He chose that culture to infuse His message, His son, and our redemption. His view is revelatory and will teach us to know Him, His path, His ways, and how to operate with a supernatural ability as Jesus did; changing culture.

As we embrace the covenant with Christ, we will begin to function out of a Jewish mindset and our choices will be full of His purpose and His will, culminating with Heaven's Kingdom established on the earth. It's simple. Operate in the same realm Jesus did, and we win. This *Shift* is a vital step.

A PERSONAL SHIFT

There is no question that from 1991 to 1995 it was a time in my life where all things flowed under an open heaven. That marvelous season was followed by twenty years of searching and frustration. Not that I didn't experience the Lord, or that I didn't trust His plan for me. Rather, I am just now beginning to understand His reasons for such dramatic change and how He moved in my life during those years. Like the people of Israel, God allowed me to taste of His presence and anointing in such a way that I would remain internally frustrated until the desire for change was so great that the mere pressure for release forced me forward. The much-needed change inside was simply to position me for what He is now accomplishing.

My personal operating system was not able to sustain the power of the open heaven God intended as we now see it. During this time of frustration, my belief system, the understanding of who God was, how He thought and what He would do, was horribly conflicted. While pastoring in Redding, God just spoke, and I obeyed. I watched situations, people and money come into a unique alignment and life flowed freely out of that power. During the twenty-year journey, I did not comprehend how the Father was going to completely transform my world; in which it, nor I, would ever be the same again.

After such an amazing season of His handiwork, transitioning back into the marketplace felt like a demotion. On autopilot, I defaulted to what felt most comfortable and a way of thinking that demanded no change. I reverted back to functioning within a system I knew how to manage; one that only allowed me to maintain. Many of us do that when unidentifiable change comes without understanding. What was God trying to do in and through me? I had experienced His new wine, the unleashing presence, within an old wineskin commonly known as my mindset. I was unable to sustain an unceasing flow of His presence without essential, personal change. This time the *Shift* needed to occur in me, not around me. Since that time, a few things have become much clearer, which may help you too.

> **The *Shift* needed to occur in me, not around me.**

The Father took me on a journey to experience a myriad of life I had never known before. This required a change in how I understood ministry, business, and people as a whole. Whenever one does not understand the 'why' of God, it can open the door to vain imagination. Personally, the length of this journey reinforced the punitive perspective I carried. It lasted far longer than I thought it would and like many of you, I walked down paths I would not choose today.

Nonetheless, God had a plan, and I was due for an overhaul! My life experience had to grow. Romans 12:1-2, speaks of presenting ourselves as a living sacrifice and in that, "be not conformed to this world, but be ye transformed by the renewing of your mind, that ye may prove what is that good, and acceptable, and perfect, will of

Tension stretches us beyond limits motivating a reach for more of God.

God." Proving His perfect will requires a converging of our choices and limited understanding with His word and directions. I needed a transformed mind that would redirect how I operated both spiritually and in the natural.

Remember, the Law paved the way for the people of God to reach for and embrace the New Covenant Jesus provided for us. So it was with me. Tension increased when the stretching grew beyond normal limits, motivating me to reach out for more of Him. Having had a taste of an open heaven hooked me, causing me to be eternally dissatisfied for anything less. Even when I no longer felt sure of who I was or where God was taking me, I longed for more of Him. The twenty-year season was merely an opportunity for my longing to increase in drastic measures, reducing my ability to lean purely on my natural gifts and talents. Recklessly abandoning myself before the King, I allowed Him to bring the necessary changes I desired and needed. He rewired my circuitry, placing in me the ability to experience a new level of intimacy and understand His new assignment for my life.

That step provided an avenue for the advancement I am now experiencing. Outward promotion is the very least of the benefits of what God brings. Housing His glory and presence is by far the greatest reward He gives. Once I began to take an aerial view, my DNA began to morph like the Hebrews experienced. I fully understand why He paved a way, through the blood of Jesus, to exercise His dominion authority. In order to properly carry the name and the purposes of His Son, a provision of wealth and influence must occur. *There had to be a Shift 'in' me before there could be one 'around' me.*

NO THANK YOU, DR. SCHOFIELD

Truly, Dr. Schofield was a man who loved God. However, in my opinion, intentionally or not, I believe this great man's influence may be responsible for much of the traditional church taking a wrong worldview. His teachings diverted modern Christianity from the path it was meant to travel. With the introduction of Cessation or Dispensationalism, the Bride of Christ has traveled many degrees in the wrong direction.

If our adversary can separate us into factions (denominations) and push us to move in opposing directions, we will never come together in unity, stay the course and finish our assignment. Make no mistake. Jesus Christ fulfilled the legal requirements concerning the Kingdom, but establishing dominion on earth is our responsibility. In 2 Corinthians 5:6-8, Paul talks about being torn by wanting to be useful here on earth, yet longing to be present with his Lord. No kidding. Who would not want to be with Jesus? Paul is conflicted because he understood, unlike Greek-influenced Christians, that we have a greater purpose than waiting on the Lord's return. It's not just about 'fire insurance.' We, like Jesus, are commissioned to tear down the high places of the enemy and releasing His power and presence, drawing others to Him. In doing so, we are made perfect, even as Christ was made perfect, bringing Jesus the reward due Him.

THERE IS ONLY ONE EXIT STRATEGY

Like Paul, I long to be with our Lord, but Jesus has other plans for now. Whether you take a position as a pre-millennialist, a post-millennialist, or an a-millennialist, you can relax. There is no need to defend any end-time eschatological beliefs. Our discussion here is not about the timing in which Jesus Christ will return. However, it *is* about what we are doing here until He does. I would enjoy a surprise departure from the pains of this life, but we are to remain focused on the prize. We are to release God's glory as we live as Christ, follow His lead and execute His directives. Don't let the adversary magnify pet theologies or doctrines and distract us from the ability to hear truth. The Father's plan started in the Garden and will not end until we, God's change agents, complete it. The cross of Christ was the path to succeed just like He did.

We are called to release God's glory in and through us as we live as Christ.

Romans 8:17f states, ". . . if children, heirs of God and joint heirs with Christ." As a sibling, we share mutually in Christ's inheritance. In other words, God has a *Family Business,* and we share in the process as well as the profits. The Father's business will be fully financed and granted legal jurisdiction to accomplish what he has set in motion for you and me since the beginning of time.

Those of us, who have allowed God's character to be forged within, will be positioned in spheres of great influence in which we did not necessarily earn the right to lead. He will dispense resources that He has reserved specifically for the strategies appointed from Heaven. It is captured in a single phrase, from the lips of Jesus himself, as He shares the parable of the nobleman who issued provision to those in business, ". . . Occupy until I come;" Luke 19:13.

THE SHIFT HAS BEGUN

Shift has begun on three key fronts. Primarily, the Bride of Christ is *shifting* back into realignment in character, demonstrated by action. As we have the mind of Christ, our daily activities will reveal the heart of God. As individuals transition, collectively the church will amalgamate, permitting the heavens to open. Not just in pockets across the world, but like clouds that form, build, continuously move and finally bring their release. Just as it was in the New Testament, a continuous infusion of Jesus' presence, love and jurisdiction will be released worldwide.

Those who have allowed God's character to be forged within, will be positioned in spheres of great influence.

Finally, as the Spirit distributes influence on those of us God has prepared to steward it, He will then unleash from His storehouse all that is needed to fund His plan. It's already evident in limited regions, but it will grow excessively. Creativity is being unleashed. Innovative ideas, inventions, and distinct methods are coming from Heaven that will produce an aroma of success and attract the world to it. They will gather to the scent of His presence, and the light of Christ will resonate from within us. The influence and essence we carry will draw individuals and tribes of people until the salvation of souls comes in, like waves on the ocean.

A REALIGNMENT IN YOU

God's alignment began with each of us when we accepted Jesus Christ as our personal Savior. However, before the church as a unit will march toward the final fulfillment of God's plan, a turning point for His purpose must take place. The journey we have been on, the refinement of our character, our values, our motives and our actions will all be redirected. It's merely a result of the Supernatural School of Stewardship we have been attending! Little did we know, when we were seeking the Father for His greatest outpouring to begin, He personally enrolled us. Remember asking God if you could just participate? You even longed for promotion, to be used in a greater measure? He has been faithful to your request. We may have preferred a different method of education, but I don't believe the outcome would have been the same. He has given each one legal access, positions of influence and the maturity to receive and handle the measure of wealth needed for the redemption of nations.

Jesus said, "If I be lifted up, I will draw all men unto me." It remains so. We are now tempered and ready to exalt Jesus in the manner He always chose; the drawing of all men unto Himself through us. On this platform, to glorify the name of Jesus, we must show forth the true character and heart of His Father. Then you are ready to graduate from the Supernatural School of Stewardship. It's time to walk in the reality of the promise described in Ephesians 1:17-23:

> "[17] I keep asking that the God of our Lord Jesus Christ, the glorious Father, may give you the Spirit[f] of wisdom and revelation, so that you may know him better. [18] I pray that the eyes of your heart may be enlightened in order that you may know the hope to which he has called you, the riches of his glorious inheritance in his holy people, [19] and his incomparably great power for us who believe. That power is the same as the mighty strength [20] he exerted when he raised Christ from the dead and seated him at his right hand

in the heavenly realms, [21] *far above all rule and authority, power and dominion, and every name that is invoked, not only in the present age but also in the one to come.* [22] *And God placed all things under his feet and appointed him to be head over everything for the church,* [23] *which is his body, the fullness of him who fills everything in every way.* ["]

THE *SHIFT*: THY KINGDOM COME, THY WILL BE DONE, ON EARTH AS IT IS IN HEAVEN!

CHAPTER FOUR

HIS STOREHOUSE FOR TRANSFER

HIS ORIGINAL INTENTIONS

Solomon makes this noteworthy statement in Proverbs 13:22b that piques the interest of most readers, but commands the attention of the devoted follower of Christ. "But the wealth of the sinner is stored up for the righteous." Stop and read that again! On the surface, it seems this comment is about money. At some level, it's all about the greenbacks. I have heard some startling teachings about Proverbs 13 based on the supposition that money would just be dropped into the bank accounts of Christ followers. Not to be flippant, I am sure there are a few recorded stories of such events.

An example of a context for such belief is Israel's departure from Egypt. You know about the story of the Hebrews liberation from slavery? As they were leaving the cities of their bondage, the Egyptians freely gave of their abundance to hurry the slaves on their way out of the country. So, we know that through unusual circumstances, God can produce wealth in an instant. However, the Hebrew word 'wealth' speaks of a comprehensive description of provision from a Biblical perspective, which I will address shortly. If not careful, what can be overlooked is the true nature of wealth, lost in part because of our limited vocabulary. Verse 22b is a far weightier promise than monetary provision, such is why we must become familiar with what a first glance can reveal!

WARNING! A LOSS IN TRANSLATION

I wish I could speak and read Hebrew really well. Yes, I did take Hebrew in college and from one of the nation's great Hebrew translators. However, like everyone else, I trudge out my Strong's Concordance along with other Bible helps to put together a reasonable view of what is being said. What has become crystal clear about this scripture, is that much is lost in translation. As we try to find English equivalents to Hebrew word values, we find that many Hebrew words, just like English, have an array of meanings depending upon the context in which the word is used. One word can mean something a little different given the circumstance. The words wealth, sinner, laid, and righteous, have powerful connotations when the right meaning is applied in the appropriate context. We need to understand what King Solomon, under the inspiration of the Holy Spirit, is saying again today.

For a two-year period while yet a teenager, I lived in a foster home where Spanish was the predominantly spoken language. What a great experience! That brief time influenced my entire life in more ways than one. To bring home a point, while living there I learned how to speak conversational Spanish. This was a language that is not taught to students in Spanish 101. Words have personality. They can expand the point one wishes to make. In 2009, I was in Nicaragua speaking at a conference for business leaders and pastors on the subject of wealth. I used a word that was easily understood by the Mexican culture in East Los Angeles, but the

Spanish spoken in Nicaragua was much different from the Spanish I was using. When I accidently commanded the group to hurry up rather than asking them if they all agreed with me. I received a room full of bewildered looks instead of a hearty "Amen," which is what I preferred they say. What an education! Similarly, Bible translators sometimes translate words literally, unless they are familiar with the context and culture it was originally written for.

THE POWER OF WORDS

In this passage, truly there are only four key words that define what Proverbs 13:22b is trying to convey. Let's dig deeper! **Warning!** *Do not skip this exercise as it is essential to the Shift that is coming.*

First Word Study—Wealth

> **WEALTH:** The common English translation of the Hebrew word 'chayil.'[1]

Here, Solomon saw the bounty of Heaven and realized the abundance the Father wanted His children to experience. There are two distinct parts to the word *wealth* in this context. First, 'chayil' means strength, efficiency and wealth; a larger understanding than just money. Secondly, He who is entrusted with such responsibility must have the fortitude to stay the course without being influenced. This is an attitude of one's heart. Such attributes are only formed through the molding of character. Character that has been tested and tried, perhaps even failed, but when refined, is entrusted with the abundance of God's storehouse where He positions you to act.

Outwardly, common words that describe wealth may include riches, goods, and substance. Inwardly, they could be defined as choices of virtue, valor, and strength. Understanding these words together enables us to correctly define the expanse of God's meaning of wealth. As the writer of Proverbs reflected on all he knew and experienced, all descriptive words applied. Accumulating financial increase, along with other tangibles, is just one form of the promise to us that should be applied!

To be successful at receiving and able to manage wealth, one must *possess the internal values* of wealth including:

VIRTUE: moral excellence

VALOR: boldness and determination in the face of danger

STRENGTH: moral power and courage.

These qualities embedded in your character will provide the intestinal fortitude to successfully live out the transfer of wealth and influence that God intends to *Shift* your direction. To appreciate all that the Father makes available to His children, we must broaden our view. Read each word in the box above and let it register deep within your spirit. Do not expect to receive the Father's abundant storehouse without learning and reflecting the characteristics of His heart. The strength forged in your character must come first. That development reminds each of us daily that **all wealth belongs to God.**

Prosperity, as explained by our culture, is about possessing resources far beyond need or desire! Some call this being rich or being richer. This level of financial security offers you the freedom to choose what you do and when you do it. Nonetheless, in this context it includes freedom with your time, freedom to dream, to work, develop, and to play.

All of that is absolutely true. However, real wealth should not be reduced to dollars and cents. True wealth is to possess values and resources to live the abundant life that was spoken of in John 10:10. God's original intentions were that man's life was never to be reduced to earning and spending.

Authentic wealth from Him involves creativity and favor with both God and man. This wealth includes authority and power, granting you the capacity to bring influence and change into people's lives. Ephesians 3:20 says, "Now to him who is able to do immeasurably more than all we ask or imagine, according to his power that is at work within us."

God is a genius beyond our imagination. Wealth to Daniel is being shut up in a Lion's den and never scratched. Creative wealth for Jesus was tax money delivered from the mouth of a fish. Wealth to Nikolah Tesla, the great Christian inventor, was an idea from heaven on how to transfer electricity without wires from Long Beach, California to Catalina Island. You see, western civilization envisions wealth as merely a bloated bank account or profitable retirement investments. Fortune to the children of God includes *courage, valor,* and *virtue* which qualifies you to handle power, authority, and influence. Imagine a spirit-led force of Kings, marketplace ministers, living out the heart of God with character, break-through inventions, and cultural advancements. We would have the "cause of heaven" uniting us together into formation, like an army the world has never known before. We become a force to be reckoned with.

Our society today honors those who have acquired riches, even if they conduct themselves with poor moral character or unscrupulous behavior. The Biblical perspective places a greater value on everything 'above' money. In this transfer, only those who demonstrate good character (virtue) and courage (valor) are

Wealth is infinitely far more than what's in your wallet.

going to be trusted to handle God's earthly resources (finances). All men, created in the image of God, were designed and intended to have available for use, Heaven's wealth in full capacity to use on the earth. As the word says in Psalm 24:1, "The earth is the Lord's and the fullness thereof." God can and will release an abundance to those who have the vision, the character, the cause, and the fortitude to use it as the Father would mandate. Wealth is infinitely far more than what's in your wallet.

FORFEITING YOUR INHERITANCE

Second Word Study—Sinner

> **SINNER**: The common English translation of the Hebrew word '*chata.*' [2]

Here is another word frequently applied with a shallow definition. The word 'sinner' can mean many things to many people, but it clearly ends up simply defined as rebellious life choices that have resulted in separation from God. As you dig deeper into the descriptive word 'sinner,' the Hebrew writer describes not only the separation sin causes from God but also the earthly consequences it produces. Sin disconnects the one who sins from all that heaven encompasses. A sinner not only loses intimacy with the Father, but the rebellious act prohibits the Father from releasing all that is available through relationship to Him.

Life was never meant to be as difficult as it has become. Post 'original sin' man has to work from the sweat of his brow, not by the power of the Spirit. Jesus modeled the life of authority and dominion that heaven provides, which is restored back to us through His death and resurrection. Deductive reasoning teaches that if something had to be restored, something had to first be lost. What was lost? Our intimacy with God and all the benefits that accompany a relationship with Him! Simply put, mankind without Christ has forfeited citizenship and access to both the natural and supernatural resources that God arranged for us to enjoy.

Does that mean then, that one who does not believe in Christ cannot acquire wealth and influence his culture? Well, they most certainly can succeed in acquiring finances and lead in places of influence. Remember the golden rule? 'He who owns the gold makes the rules'!

Interestingly, Biblical principles are universal and subsist with a non-optional cause and effect that does not favor those who know and receive Christ versus those who choose not to. That measure of success can be earned by the sweat of their brow, also known as human efforts. Anyone can benefit from God's uncompromising principles when they are applied. However, that is not dominion, influence or favor issued by the Holy Spirit. History depicts many great world leaders, but I don't recall one that resembled anything like Jesus. Nor has anyone understood and changed an entire culture like the early disciples. With a citizenship in heaven, access and intimacy with the Father is natural. You have been given jurisdiction from heaven to prosper here on earth.

UNUSED HEAVENLY RESOURCES

Third Word Study—Stored

> **STORED:** A common English translation
> of the Hebrew word 'tsaphan.' [3]

The Father created resources for the work He commissioned. As a citizen of Heaven's economy, we can access all renewable resources. Not just renewable in a natural sense, but in supernatural realms as well. So, where is this bounty reserved by Father God for His children to use in Jesus' name? If you live without having a relationship with God and block access to all He has prepared, because of deliberate choice, what happens to *that* stored stockpile of resources?

The answer to that question is captured in the definition of the word 'tsaphan' or stored up. Let's see how 'stored' fits into the whole scheme of things. It means to place in reserve, or hoard up for another use at another time. Descriptive synonyms bestow a broader view of this word and include 'privy, to protect and to keep secret.' The Father holds in His reserve, possessions to use, which He created for anyone who would set their hearts to carry out His purposes. In fact, possessions that some have forfeited are held in reserve for someone else to use. Everything has been 'stored up' for another's use, at another time and this my friend, is the time!

In a nutshell, 'Stored up' means to put in reserve for the right time, the right people, and the right purpose!

A LEGAL RIGHT

Fourth Word Study—Righteous

> **RIGHTEOUS:** The common English translation of the Hebrew word 'tsaddiyq.' [4]

The book of Romans declares "There is none righteous, no not one." Basic Kingdom truth speaks that you can never be in right relationship with God by your own efforts, or because you were made in God's likeness. Giving your life to Jesus Christ not only pays the debt of sin, but it also translates you from the Kingdom of darkness into the Kingdom of God. Wow, what an exchange!

The word 'just' or 'righteous' signifies being in a right relationship. The inference being that righteousness is a restored position with the Father through Jesus Christ. In this context, 'righteous' means just, righteous or lawful. That last word, 'lawful,' is more significant than you know. When someone gives their life to Jesus Christ, they enter into a legal adoptive state with the Father. Literally, they are now part of His family. The only way to be legally suitable in heaven is to be adopted into the family of God through the blood of Christ.

Acts 17:28 says, "In Him we live, move, and have our being." A restored relationship opens up access to heaven, but also to its amenities, including the resources and power to do the Father's bidding. From the beginning, God has had a plan already in place. He intended for the plan to be executed by one nation. His nation— the Kingdom of God.

Righteousness guarantees you possess the right and legal relationship with the Father which enables you by His spirit to exercise the fullness of His supply for His intended cause. Now that key words are defined, let's be about the Father's business and allow our hearts and minds to grasp King Solomon's scripture; what he envisioned, what he wanted us to see and, like him, experience!

AN INSIDE PERSPECTIVE

It often crosses my mind when I read a transforming thought in Scripture, what did the writer want us to see or know? What part of God's heart was being revealed to the person with the pen? Sometimes, I wish I was standing there when the writer spoke of and wrote down the words of God.

I have a friend, now with the Lord, named David Russet. He was just an astounding man! He was a scientist with NASA, an inventor, and a builder; truly a 'Renaissance Man.' He was one of those who seemingly could do it all. Starting in 2001 and until the time of his death, we met together to fellowship and pray two and even three times a week. At his memorial, lots of people shared anecdotes about the diverse interests he pursued throughout his lifetime. While listening, I gave thought on how truly privileged I was. During our frequent meetings, David would share with me, in great depth, many of the topics that I heard people lightly reminiscing about. My heart raced as I listened to them. Here is why.

These folks were sharing their 'cliff-note' versions of the conversations they had with David. It was all kind, yet tepid and understated. In reality, my friend understood significant dimensions about the scientific measure and the Scripture, which came from reading sixty chapters of the Bible every day! No wonder the Father shared His insights with David. These dear friends merely had an unfocused snapshot of a man, who not only studied science as a vocation, but integrated it and interpreted revelation through his daily consumption of the Word and time spent with his Father.

I am sure I did not know the background of every story shared that day, but I embraced my relationship with an appreciation of the depth of David's heart that seemed evident, at least to me, that perhaps others did not. I realized although they were 'aware' of him, they did not genuinely know this man I had grown to love and value so deeply.

As I mentioned earlier, Solomon explained and experienced a deeper comprehension of God's Kingdom and intentions than we may have fully embraced. He did not have a cliff note understanding of the vast love and desire the Father had to give all He has for us.

All He stored up is ready to be transferred to His children. Perhaps it is the greatest transfer of wealth ever known. This *Shift* is quite simple. The riches, both internal and external, that were forfeited by others who rejected God, have been stored up in reserve for those who have been reinstated, realigned, and are in a right relationship with Him.

C H A P T E R   F I V E

CRITICAL MASS

SCIENTIFIC PROOF AND SUPERNATURAL TRUTH

S cientific terms used to validate spiritual truths appeal to me. I am not the first to use 'Critical Mass' to authenticate a point. Natural science is a window to understand spiritual activity. Here is an example that may help.

During the Katrina disaster, the levies that held back the oceans finally gave way, when the pressure of wind and water exceeded their purpose and function to hold it back. This is a perfect physical example of the spiritual climate we are in today. The weight of our current social economic circumstances is causing the levies of previous choices to give way to them. Current crisis become the opportunity for a supernatural *Shift* that effectively enables the bride of Christ to take her place in the society she should have always known.

One scientist that caught my attention is David Van Koevering, a quantum physicist, who uncovers an exceptional correlation between the world of science and the Bible. Many of his discoveries present Critical Mass as much a spiritual reality as a physical one. Van Koevering, with over six hundred patents, has discovered unbelievable insights on matter and frequency; both significantly playing a factor in the activity of God. One noteworthy discovery is how matter holds memory. Can you imagine what the walls in any given building could tell us? If we could look over God's shoulder at the blueprint, perhaps we would see how the juncture, both natural and supernatural, can create an opportunity for the inevitable *Shift* that is presently in motion.

We are at a crossroads where Critical Mass will be achieved on two essential fronts, economically and socially – virtually at the same time. There is a collision of value systems occurring between the Kingdom of God and the current world systems. The Father, in his exceptional, brilliant way, has used this Critical Mass to bring inevitable change to accomplish heaven's purposes.

A MOMENT OF CHANGE

> **CRITICAL MASS:** the amount necessary or sufficient to have a significant effect or to achieve a given result.

The book of Revelation, Chapter 5 verse 8, articulates well the four living creatures and the twenty-four elders falling down before the Lamb. Each one has a harp and are holding golden bowls full of incense, which are the prayers of God's people. Those priceless prayers are presented before God. Another angel, who has a golden censer, comes and stands at the altar. He was given incense to offer, the collected prayers of all God's people, on the golden altar and in front of God's throne. Smoke from the incense, together with the prayers, went up before Him from the angel's hand.

I propose that Critical Mass is reached when an accumulation of those prayers fill heavens bowl and rise as incense before God. Those bowls are filled with our worship and prayers. Once filled to the brim, the volume alone spills out, demanding the attention of the Father as it's presented for an incense offering to Him. Without question, it is our prayers that tip the scales on behalf of His people. God is compelled to respond to this significant amount of prayer and will bring corrective adjustments. Change is the subject of this chapter! Critical Mass: the amount necessary to culminate to a level that initiates the change, expected or not.[1]

In the book of Genesis, Chapter 6, the story of Noah is a prime example. The collective amount of rebellion against God purely demanded a response from Him. His determination to modify the population, resulted in a global flood. Just to be clear, I am deliberately making dramatic statements about the momentum of certain factors that are cataclysmic in producing this much-needed *Shift* within our culture. Not only is a metamorphosis needed within our social and economic landscape, but that *Shift* is caused by components within the body of Christ and our world structure.

As David Van Koevering validated in his proven methods, both the tangible world and the intangible spiritual dimensions work together. The *Shift* we are currently experiencing is a culmination of both. Insurmountable evidence points towards a timeliness for the Body of Christ to expand the Kingdom of God and step into this *Shift*, with confidence to lead the way. Momentum is erupting. Intentional or not, the consequence of our choices and actions have been heaped up before God, demanding His hand to move. Something has to turn around.

SHIFT FACTORS ...

Jesus promulgates about His generation and their inability to comprehend even the simplest indicators like weather. How is it they will understand the appointed signs of their time? Perhaps that is the challenge for most Believers to appreciate what is occurring in their lifetime, but more so, what is their personal role to play. I Chronicles 12:32 clearly identifies one Tribe, out of the twelve, who clearly knew their role. "Issachar, men who understood the times and knew what Israel should do." Humorous to say, there has always been a remnant of God's people who both understand the times and have the mettle to embrace their duty and make a difference. In this strategic *Shift,* those roles are being defined even as I write.

We are at a tipping point of change. Are you ready to fulfill your part?

Look closer at the state of our world and the economic place in which we find ourselves, as well as, the spiritual climate of the Bride of Christ. It is no secret that an intervention is necessary to facilitate breakthrough. We are at a tipping point where the scales will *Shift* in one direction or another. God is positioned and ready to unleash His 'wealth' in the full context of the word. Subsequently, we will now see the scales of power and authority *Shift*. Specific factors are intensifying and will determine the *Shift*. The question you need to answer is, "Are you ready to fulfill your part and make a difference?" It's one thing to know what is happening and even what may be needed, but sadly not many will choose to become *agents of change.* The Father has been searching for those with fortitude, those He can trust, who not only understand the need, but like the Tribe of Issachar, know what to do and does it. In case you don't know, ask yourself, "What kind of evidence unveils the 'signs of the times'?"

A KEEN SENSE FOR THE OBVIOUS

W.C. Fields, a famous comedian, once said to someone trying to wax eloquent, "You have a keen sense for the obvious," meaning what they believed to be a guarded insight, was in reality apparent to all. Our culture is desperately poised for a course correction. The deafening cry that can be heard in this vacuum is waiting to be filled.

Four significant factors mark the signs for such a change; Prevailing Mindsets, the Economy, the Winds of Change and the Bible. These four conditions are rapidly coming together, *Shifting* what was into what will be. This is an Issachar opportunity for our generation to understand the times, know what to do and even better, to go do it!

FACTOR 1 — *Prevailing Mindsets*

Early one morning, while listening to a national news program, I caught a glimpse of American attitudes and concerns. The highlighted stories all seemed to have a growing theme. There appeared to be an increasing pattern of fear, distrust and more significantly, a disillusionment with the reins of government, health care, immigration, unifying the country and the overall condition of our times. It was evident these were not fleeting comments, but represented growing and fixed mindsets of dissatisfaction and discontent. Established thinking, once rooted in the heart of man, becomes hard to change.

Although President Trump has stepped up to rally people together. His goal was to unify the hearts of a nation and create positive change. Yet seasoned mindsets, groups and parties continue to push back because of beliefs and agendas, regardless of an increase in morale, national security, and economic growth strengthening a nation's financial position for this generation and others to follow.

When attitudes prevail as they currently do, it creates an environmental chasm. Whether it's a positive correction or a negative one depends on followers of Christ becoming the activist that facilitates all God desires. Significant adjustments are already in motion. These changes will be navigated successfully by the wisdom of Godly leaders, or a persistent march against them will drive us into deeper trouble. A desperation for Jesus and Him alone, must anchor within us. Our trust cannot be established anywhere else. Are you, His chosen, ready?

Many of the events of recent history were experienced by Israel thousands of years before we were born. Now, it is repeating. Uncertainty about life and where it's headed creates a unique void, one that will be filled. Our cultural container is empty of moral values and standards that once bubbled over. Values like respect, civility, the nuclear family and embracing life over convenience, exhibited by 40+ years of legalized abortion. What about the entertainment arena? Even the technological advances we enjoy have subrogated relationships and intimacy through texting, email, and social media. Current alt-values convey anger, rudeness, lying, selfishness, intolerance and callousness. These are trademarks we now witness on a daily basis.

There is a grievous loss of respect for authority and leadership today. In this current climate, political conflict has become filled with insults and abuse. It's common and even applauded to discredit leaders and 'look for the dirt'. Individuality trumps unity. Integrity has often been replaced with greed. Instant gratification has displaced the fruit of long-term satisfaction and the pleasure of doing one's job well. Entertainment has replaced enterprise. If we measure our values by where people spend their money, then being amused is more important than being engaged. It reminds me of the Roman Empire before its final collapse. This short list defines the substance of a *Shift* occurring at a rate that can no longer be ignored.

In 2011, John Boehner, the newly elected Speaker of the House, was interviewed by a news broadcaster. In a dialogue regarding the greatness of America and the opportunities that we offer to people around the world, Mr. Boehner shared his 'American Dream'. He explained how he began life as an impoverished child of an immigrant and the journey his family took raising twelve children. Mr. Boehner recalled his first job working at grandpa's bar at the young age of eight. He pursued his dream funding his own way through college. The American dream paid off, as he became Speaker of the House of the United States of America. This leader was so concerned about the state our economy and culture it is in, that he was moved to tears. It was a moving story that stirred the memories of those who remember the work, the opportunity and the value system we once held. Although Congress received a great focus from the media, like all other staple institutions, it still has offered little comfort and even fewer answers.[2]

Listen carefully. Sustenance, family provision, morality, kindness, gender identity and wavering faith, to name a few, are matters we have collectively turned away from. Today as confusion, crisis and uncertainty soar like a rocket, *we must face them*. People want change, but what will be offered in exchange: disparity or assurance? At this crucial intersection of circumstances, personal and national values that we have allowed to encroach into our culture as normative, are now being called to account; especially in the courts of Heaven.

ON A COLLIDING PATH

Not only are individual mindsets revealed by the nature of our choices, but mindsets form collectively in people groups, cultures and even within the Body of Christ. We currently have a great divide. It is interesting how words change in meaning or application and evolve over time. One can rightly define theology as the 'study of' God. Over time it has morphed to become the various perspectives about God, about man and even about history.

The mere knowledge of theology in itself creates a conflict in the mind of man. For in our attempt to understand the multi-facets of God, the complexity creates conflict in trying to determine which theological interpretation might be the correct one. Thus disunity, confusion and conflict continue to grow, so much so that the Body of Christ could miss a generational destiny. Prevailing theological mindsets (not worth further discussion or definition thereof) could unthinkably immobilize the Church at her greatest moment.

Although I have given my life to the study of God's word, for the first time as an adult, I am no longer impressed, nor fulfilled, with the 'study of' God as I once was. For the Lord has awakened my spirit to the present; here now and today! Not only in the course of a climate full of tension and uncertainty, but in the midst of joy, expectancy and enthusiasm, I must experience Christ Jesus today! He, who is revealed by the Word He has written.

FACTOR 2 — *It's the Economy, Stupid*

Typically, in the hearts of unredeemed man, most return to a core issue of money. Greenbacks, gold, oil and gas and the economy are the hot topics today. Yet, there remains a preoccupation with decline, government subsidy, the growing issue of immigration and often mere survival. It makes sense that the heart of man is fearfully fixed on the instability of his provision. It is impossible to listen to the news and not predominantly hear about conflict, insult which feeds fear and breeds instability. Even in the strongest of economic advancement, those issues feed a poverty spirit. Fear of loss and lack are common emotions in the American soul for good reasons. It was just a few years ago we experienced double-digit unemployment, shuttered businesses, mortgage foreclosures and spiraling bankruptcies. Consumer debt was off the charts and past leaders ran amuck with lavish increase in government supplementation. That volcano erupted and it will happen again.

In 2009, Russian and Chinese leaders called for a new global currency. They were determined to discontinue American greenbacks as the currency of commodity trade. And they still are.[3] That is an indictment of our economic status and an alarming wake-up call! All of America realize that should a 'gold standard' return, Americas economy will *Shift* dramatically. In 2010, Hollywood released *Wall Street: Money Never Sleeps.*[4] That movie depicts events in the economy that transpired earlier in the twenty-first century. *I remember it very well.* During that time, I was deeply involved in the financial markets, as our company was purchased and financed by parties representing one of the banks that was literally sold for pennies on the dollars during the crash. Not only did the economy crash, my world I had diligently worked and planned for, also crashed. That crisis providentially ended the financial upgrade we had planned and forced me to turn in another direction.

For the last thirty years a storm has been developing over America. Our nation has long been considered a 'kingpin' in the world's economy, as well a superpower. The phrase, "As America goes, so goes the world," is still very true. The banking fiasco I mentioned earlier, put the skids to my business plan. Literally overnight. At that time, I could not foresee the demise of the business I had been building for two years as a window God opened to launch me into future opportunities. It was during that *Shift* that God disclosed to me, not only what was coming, but He also positioned me to prosper by redirecting me in areas I am to occupy.

Looking back now, I can see His handiwork. During the moment, in the middle of crisis, it was frustratingly obscure. The Father not only put me in alignment with the banking industry related to the real estate collapse and foreclosures, but He ushered me into arenas I never fathomed I could lodge in, to establish His Kingdom. The personal change I experienced forged a renewed mentality and mission. He made me a new man, naturally and spiritually. Not only was there a restoration of all God had promised, but a significant advancement for His Kingdom. In Proverbs 16:9 it says, "A man's heart plans his course, but the Lord determines his steps." His word never fails.

HE WHO OWNS THE GOLD MAKES THE RULES

Have you ever heard that phrase before? Of course you have! This is another reality that is confirmed by thousands of years of history! All wars are typically about money, power and sometimes religion. Nonetheless, every transaction involves currency of one nature or another. This is all the more reason why God must equip a generation to understand His heart and views of money and how He implements strategy. Oh, I am sure there are those who believe, even without God's involvement, they can use their finances to influence and shape history. On the surface that may look entirely true, except for two words ... *but God.*

There is a plan afoot for the redistribution of power, money and position within culture. I believe that the adversary of our soul runs a parallel plan to the Father's for this reallocation. At this moment, both sides are amassing an arsenal for this climactic moment in history. Of epic importance, one must engage and know the Father more deeply. Only out of intimacy He will reveal what will happen in current times and how we are to function under His direction within them. Paul Bilheimer, in his book *Destined for the Throne,*[5] wisely addresses our purpose and the principles God uses to credential us to rule and reign in His Kingdom. Thus, we can "occupy until He comes."

As stated in Haggai 2:6-9, when the Lord comes to display His authority, He will do so in the natural realm through the shaking of the heavens and the earth. But verse six specifically states, "The silver is mine and the gold is mine, and the glory of this present house will be greater than the former house." If you believe that common colloquialism of the influence of gold mentioned earlier, then read Haggai chapter two again. It clarifies the Father's ability to effortlessly deal with every financial tsunami.

> " **The glory of this present house will be greater than the former house"**
>
> Haggai 2:9

The *Shift* in motion is deliberate. Selah. Even the influence billionaires worldwide believe they have, does not possess the authority to bring about the kind of change our Father has intended. As stated multiple times in scripture, "The earth is the Lord's and the fullness thereof." And that, my friend, is the end of it. Fullness includes resources, governments and all of creation. Even profane arenas that man may stake his claim to, are made in God's image and remain under His command. Read Isaiah, Chapter 40, as he characterizes nations and landmasses of the world described from heaven's point of view. Those who possess anything, are allowed to do so under the auspices of God's rule. Fittingly, the adage is literally true, "He who owns the gold *does* make the rules." God owns it all and He sets the rules.

The Word is filled with business principles to practice and they are inseparably knit around the spiritual values of character and honor, regardless of the condition of any economy. There is nothing new coming to us that God has not taken notice of and His Word tells us, He has already prepared us to be overcomers.

Perhaps just as I experienced an abrupt, even unwelcomed, course correction, it's most likely the current changes of your life where the Father is directing you to peer through a different window and pay attention to how He is answering your requests. I propose He is pointing you towards greater places and positions for you to walk in. While the majority of the world's population sees the natural evidence of a *Shift* and feels despair listening to the media; take note of the climate around you. What is the Father speaking in your circumstance?

FACTOR 3 — *The Winds of Change*

We have the mind of Christ, the Word of God and the power of the Holy Spirit. We are temples of the Holy Spirit carrying His presence and all that He entails to every people group; Ethnos. Literally, we are Holy Ghost mobile homes. Historically during times in conflict or disunity, the 'church', as we have known it, will default to former patterns or habits. A resurge in teaching the 'soon return of Christ' emerges, looking like escapism that breeds fear. Instead of Jesus' return being expressed with anticipation and joy, it becomes a route to avoid our present responsibilities and the opportunity to advance His Kingdom. Another prevailing tendency is to become myopic. We turn inward and isolated; focusing on the refinement of spiritual gifts and the quality of life within the four walls of the culture we live in. But the winds of change are blowing.

There is a large exodus within the four walls of the traditional church gatherings. Approximately one-third of professing Christians no longer attend weekly services. The average amount of time a family commits to a local assembly is now about eighteen months. As well, those who confess Christ outside the corporate structure, seem to be forming a syncretistic view of God. Distrusting the division from within the body of Christ and therefore, navigating through life without a firm Biblical direction. Many 'blend the best' of all the voices they hear and end up victims of deception. It's strong in the region I live in; very strong.

How can we reach the world with a serious dysfunction growing in and amongst His own? The power of the Holy Spirit has been given, enabling us to model *who* He is, wherever we go. However, the message has become diluted as many within the Body of Christ have focused their attention on lack, powerlessness, and escape. The winds of change are blowing in our direction. These are spiritual weather patterns of change that will penetrate the climate around us. God is moving us into exactly the right scenarios, creating conditions to result in the *Shift*. Instead of trying to outrun the wind, let us unite and see where the breath of God is carrying us. Courageously investigate all that God is showing you, His change activists. Then stand still and embrace the wind. Watch the waters separate so you can cross your dead sea. Jesus is being released through you.

DOUSED WITH COLD WATER

Back in the year 2000, while still pastoring, I reentered the marketplace. One day, while completing a financial transaction with a powerful attorney, the air was suddenly filled with obscene, foul language. Words I had not heard in a very long time. This was not just cursing, but despicable words that stunned me. Thank goodness for the game face I had developed as a baseball pitcher. Although I did not show it, hearing such words was like a cup of cold water being thrown in my face. I had been so isolated in my 'Christian' world that I no longer recognized the culture I thought I was serving. Another person in the room, who was a part of the church congregation I was leading, immediately blurted out, "That was a great sermon on Sunday, Pastor."

The attorney's countenance turned ashen. His language and the revelation of my occupation should not have phased him, but what we did not know, was he was the son of a minister and had walked away from his relationship with Christ, when he was impacted by His presence as a young man. He was dumbfounded that I had not reacted to his eruption of profanity. Apparently, he had been accustomed to experiencing reactions from others in pastoral leadership. He was unable to reconcile my vocation in the mortgage industry along with being a Pastor. It seems we in the culture of the church, have become a subculture that is easily detected. The attorney and I were able to forge a great friendship, and we met for coffee weekly. I enjoyed those times and by the way that relationship led to his decision to reconnect with the Father and his spiritual heritage. He made eternal decisions, all because I did not give off an 'air' of spiritual offense to his behavior.

Within every man is a natural desire to connect to our Father, to succeed and to prosper. People are open to listen attentively to those who exhibit the heartbeat of God. A right heart, full of the Spirit, is the model that He embedded in the 'mobile homes' we were created to be.

FACTOR 4 — *The Bible Always Tells Me So*

The longer I live the more dependent I become on the Father's personage, His word and His nature, especially when I need to understand what He is doing and how to navigate the currents of change. During the time Kings ruled over Israel in the books of 1 Samuel through 2 Chronicles, God's chosen, as a nation, experienced just about everything we experience today. Specifically within their culture, they faced economic changes accompanied by moral decline. The same dynamic reversals occurred then. Prosperity to poverty, national security to upheaval and international position and respect to disdain and disregard. Fortunately, we have not yet declined to the levels the children of Israel experienced. Exile. However, today's mindsets are leaning in the same direction much like they did in the book of Kings.

As a nation, we are not God's chosen people per se, nor are we avowing Christianity as our standard. Regardless, there is still a great presence of God and His Kingdom within our borders. There are enough followers of Christ here to make the difference He expects us to make; after all, he changed the world with only 12 good men. Similarly, like the people of Israel, we too are experiencing moments where God shows up in supernatural, power-changing encounters. Even in regards to finances and political influence. Both historically and presently, we are acting and reacting to the pressures and developments that we face. It is merely history repeating itself. If we are willing to observe what God said and did, then we can clearly identify how it will occur again. Specifically, if the body of Christ does not take its rightful place in unity and fully move in the direction He leads, it will not fare well.

MOVING IN MOTION WITH HIM

Everything we needed yesterday, today or tomorrow we find written in His word, shut up in the bones of men, looking for release. In Jeremiah 20:9, the author speaks to the calling within saying, "But his word was in mine heart as a burning fire shut up in my bones." Reading the story of Jeremiah is to discover that he was a man who had lived in Israel during one of its tumultuous seasons. Critical Mass here, was one of a personal nature. Regardless of the external on goings that may gain momentum, it is evident in the Word that God always starts with a personal, internal path of refinement, which then leads to an external corporate *Shift*.

The Bride of Christ is dissatisfied with the neutrality of traditional church.

The Holy Spirit has been stirring many of us, with an inferno of passion for His presence and purpose to be displayed. For over a decade, this fervor has been intensifying within men and women of God and His fragrance is emanating into all facets of our world. Critical Mass has become personal. The Body of Christ is ignited within. They are dissatisfied with the neutrality of what church has become and the lack of power evidenced by a continual decline. A righteous remnant is taking dominion as their passion grows. What does that really mean? How does one live in the fullness of 'all-authority' that leaks out every day at work, within their family and upon a community?

In the year 1992, while building the new Bethel Church on the 71-acre parcel in Redding, the Lord asked me to do three very unique things. First, put up flags of each nation along the road leading up to the main facility and name the road "Avenue of the Nations" (see the Gallery of Photos) as a prophetic act for reaching the nations. Secondly, at the bottom of the hill, build four pads to establish and grow businesses on the property. And lastly, build a sports field to provide 'community' for those in our city to be drawn to and participate in softball, soccer, and flag football leagues on the grounds. These were sheer prophetic acts of obedience. Often when God calls you to participate in prophetic acts, the end result may not be known or seen right away. However, the burning desire in my bones made way to the passions that grew outside my understanding as I desired to please the Father. I had no idea that when the Lord told me to create a street that visually represented all nations of the world. It was a natural act that would *literally* draw nations *to* Redding. I merely wanted the world to know Him and I wanted the Bride to affect the world like Jesus did. I thought we were to send people out to the nations, but He intended to bring the nations to us. It's history, or better yet, 'His-story' now. The revival atmosphere has drawn people from all over the planet to Redding to experience more of Christ.

Critical Mass for *Shift* in the Body of Christ begins in the heart of one person at a time. Then it multiplies until a massive army march in cadence with His intended transition for us. Spiritual momentum ignites *within* where genuine renewal first takes place. Once you are saturated, it will spill out on others, cascading like water flooding into your community. At that level, neither the individual nor the community is ever depleted of the necessary resources He has. It's the overabundance that draws attention and influences adjustments for change.

It was the passion of God within my bones to do everything He directed, including the transfer of the original Cross that was placed in front of the sanctuary. A symbol of building upon the former. Why do you think in John 15:19 Jesus speaks about being *in* the world, but not *of* the world? He knew we were meant to be *present in every facet of* our world. Only modern structure holds the belief that once someone is born-again, they 'leave' the world and join an exclusive team. God never intended for the Body of Christ to separate themselves from places and people we are called to love and influence.

PERFECT TIMING

In this critical moment of time, there appears to be two dimensions simultaneously gaining momentum, the natural and spiritual. Perhaps these dimensions are even running parallel to each other for a short time. Both are moving at such a pace that sheer energy will force a responsive *Shift*. As stated earlier in this chapter, we observed the prayers of the saints calling out for God to respond. This aggressive movement of prayer and worship that strategically has been orchestrated all over the world, is the reason Critical Mass is growing so rapidly. Not only has it placed a demand before the throne, but this corporate request has opened up fresh revelation to God's people and catapulted those who have been poised and prepared to take the glory of His presence everywhere they go. Everything is about to be challenged. Watch closely, the Body of Christ will disclose the glory of heaven like He intended we would.

Critical aggregate is also growing within our natural society, where extreme frustration concerning recent events has not played out very favorably. Tension about the economy, government and world events, along with abysmal morality, is at an all-time strain. Change is inevitable. The bowls of social and cultural pressure are filling up and, like the prayers of the saints, demanding a response.

Understanding the properties of matter, one knows that, "Two pieces of matter cannot occupy the same space at the same time." The natural and spiritual events taking place today are not isolated, nor can they operate independent of each other. These two worlds will either converge with harmonious success, or collide with a discordant outcome. The timing is not left to circumstance, but exactly in alignment with God's strategic plan. It is the creative way in which God is preparing all of us to rise up into His royal place of authority in our world. When two masses accelerate toward each other, one of them has to yield. These two kingdoms will converge at the right time, in the right way, as human history is walking directly into the path of God's glory.

ACCELERATED MOVEMENT

Writing from this vantage point, it's clear these two points of Critical Mass will not be able to coexist. Wrap it any way you want, things are just not at their best and are getting worse. Political leaders are trying desperately to keep their finger in the hole of the dike, but the hole is expanding. All our technological advances have been both a blessing and a curse. The information age has created opportunity for instant news and instant access, yet has made privacy nearly obsolete. Just log onto your computer and select one search engine; Google, Yahoo, MSN – it's like an unfolding soap opera. Everyone gets to watch everything! Sadly, this has created a dizzying roller coaster ride that does no good to the human heart. People are looking for the answers. They are searching for truth and security that could bring some understanding, or solution, to the chaos they feel.

On one level, it's exciting to watch. Still disillusionment is becoming widespread. There is a rapidly growing increase of men selfishly looking after their own interest. As stated repeatedly in the book of Judges ". . .and every man did what was right in his own eyes." The self-absorption is growing with accelerated energy. The spiritual and the natural are coming to an intersection in time where convergence cannot be avoided. It reminds me of the late 1960's and early 1970's when American youth no longer trusted the corporate world, nor where the government was leading this nation. God's timely answer, prepared in advance for our arrival, was The Jesus Movement. Tens of thousands of disenchanted youth were ushered into the Kingdom of God and the culture *Shifted* following that event. Yes, that is right, the Jesus Movement ushered in the political transformation of America!

Church leaders like Loren Cunningham, Chuck Smith, Bill Bright, Mario Murillo, Tony Salerno and others, rallied America's youth to lead a different cause, trust a change of heart and live with new mission and focus. The Father, with accelerated velocity, has yet again built into His ranks the response and answer to an opposing Critical Mass of economic upheaval, political unrest and cold, unbelieving hearts. Jesus was and always will be, the answer for our world today.

Not only has God provided answers, but He has prepared His Body to be the Change Agent; moving with extraordinary momentum to advance this transfer and bring Him the spoils. Consistent with His character and nature, God has arrived early and prepared the spiritual *Shift* bringing restoration and metamorphosis in even greater volume than the Jesus Movement did. These are all in proportion to our generation's even greater needs.

SOARING WITH EXTRAORDINARY MOMENTUM

What happens when the *Shift* exceeds that which we can manage? Something supernatural occurs. Whether it is the thrust that forges change, or the propulsion of forces beyond our eyesight. The cataclysmic adventure will feel like a 'lift off' as your wheels come off the ground and you experience forces that guide you to sensational heights. Where is the stage set for such an act of God? Just as in the book of Acts, the journey was not within the four walls of man's structure known as 'the church'. *Shift* occurred in everyday life, during the daily exchange of conversation and business transactions.

But this time God is bringing greater strategies to enhance our natural abilities. Not only is the economic stage set for the extraordinary to occur, but Christ's followers are entering the marketplace with God's strategy for revolutionary change. Momentum is not a solo event. This occurrence will ultimately be reached when corporate convergence is achieved. This will not be an incorporated entity, but individual groups of Christ's followers uniting together in their city, full of vision, invading every aspect of their community, government, education, media, religion, family units, the marketplace, arts and entertainment.

Right now in Decatur Alabama, there is a group of about 100 business people who meet weekly to collectively seek the heart of God on how their careers and influence can work together for cultural change. Another business group in San Antonio Texas, has already set up a legal entity to glean off the first-fruits of their financial profits to invest into new startups the Father is going to birth through them. There are also groups in Raleigh, NC; Jacksonville, FL; Kansas City, MO; Elk River, MN; Portland, OR; San Jose, CA; Davenport Iowa and Virginia Beach, VA which are actively building the Kingdom through the marketplace. These and many more leaders are realizing the foundation has already been laid. While seeking their assignments, they are preparing for the assembling of heaven's amalgamated movement here upon the earth. Planted all over the world, people are poised and available to be God's Change Agents. With unique talents, businesses, callings and relationships, these groups are in alignment with local leadership and excited to be a part of a momentous convergence to bring about global change for Jesus.

The Scriptures speak of the preponderance effect and power of unity. Nothing can stop a force that is in one accord. NOTHING! When the frequencies come together, it facilitates accelerated speed, just like light does. Spiritual unity is subject to the will and to faith. As unity grows and achieves Critical Mass, extraordinary velocity will emerge everywhere. The collection of personal goals and visions, merging into a unified force, will have to be reckoned with!

GALLERY OF PHOTOS

Elected January 15, 1984. On March 4, 1984 Pastor Larson
stepped into the pulpit answering the call of His own prayers.

The Mountain Calls Out
This image was taken before construction on April 17, 1993.

Ground Breaking Dedication on NEW Bethel Facility
933 College View Drive, Redding, CA.

Laying Foundations
1993

Steel Framing: This was originally to be a multi-purpose facility.
Plans for a full sanctuary were already in the making.

Parking lot filled with building supplies!

Pastor Raymond Larson—Hard hat and all!

1993

Opening Sunday
A line up to get in the new facility: October 1993.

A Full House (View from the church looking out)
October 1993. Shortly after we began holding two services!

View from the parking lot looking toward the church.

Avenue of the Nations
I thought we were sending to the nations, little
did I know the Father had other plans.

Pastor Raymond Larson
Bethel Church Dedication Sunday, December 1993.

An Abundance of Rain!
His provision for our church.

Saturday, December 18, 1993
Redding Record Searchlight

1-acre facility with special events

This aerial view shows Bethel Church's new home, which is set on more than 70 acres.

Record Searchlight Coverage December 18, 1993.
An aerial view of the mountain!

Bethel Church's parking lot is packed with vehicles during a recent service.

Affecting the City of Redding. It is God's design that we steward His character, grow in relationship and reveal Jesus Christ to the nations. It begins in your home town. When Bethel Church expanded in 1993, there was discipleship, relationship, and fruit.

Liberty Christian High School student Rose Uchibori, left, participates in a recent Wednesday night youth worship ser at Bethel Church in Redding, where the youth group has grown from eight teens to between 200 and 500 in four years.

Teens drop drugs for God

Conference focuses on conversions

■ Youth pastor Scott Anderson talked during the youth violence prevention conference about the difference God's love can make in people's lives.

By Candace L. Brown
R-S staff reporter

Bethel Church's youth group, one program featured during this week's youth violence prevention conference, has reached gang members and other at-risk teen-agers in the community.

Dave Harris remembers standing in front of the mirror buttoning a purple shirt on the day his life changed forever.

"I was thinking, I haven't smoked anything, I haven't drunk anything and my pager hasn't gone off," the 21-year-old Redding resident recalled.

Harris, then an 18-year-old drug dealer, was on his way to church — a rare occurrence for the Enterprise High School graduate, who averaged between 50 and 100 calls a day on his pager from potential customers.

"They had a testimony service where people were talking about what God was doing in their lives and it really just became real to me — that God was moving in people's lives and that I was wasting my life," he said.

"There I was, a drug dealer in church with his pager on and I was sitting there with my knees shaking and my eyes gushing. I was just bawling like a little baby."

It was Oct. 10, 1993, the day Harris gave his heart to God and gave up his drugs, pipe and pager.

"He's a great example of what our program's about," said Scott

Scott Anderson

See BETHEL, B-3

Scott Anderson, youth pastor for Bethel Church was a magnet for Jesus Christ. Pastor Larson recruited Scott from Illinois when Bethel's youth group was approximately 8 teens. Following Pastor Larson's leadership of building relationship within the City of Redding, Scott Anderson joined the Youth Violence prevention board.

This article shares the story of a former drug dealer David Harris, who gives His testimony of finding Christ at a youth meeting at Bethel Church, where he gave his life to Jesus Christ on October 10, 1993. The youth group of 8 kids, grew to an average of 300-500 teenagers seeking to know Jesus Christ every Wednesday night.

When the youth of the City are coming to your doors, trading drugs for Jesus, that is transformation! We are to grow where we are planted and the fruit will be a harvest!

Continued from B-1

Anderson, youth pastor of Bethel Church in Redding, where Harris and his wife, Jennifer, attend services. "Kids that life basically ripped off and destroyed who found the hope that is in God."

Anderson, 32, addressed a crowd of several hundred people at the Redding Convention Center on Thursday in a conference sponsored by the Youth Violence Prevention Council. He talked about instilling hope in young people, many of whom turn to drugs or gangs in a search for meaning.

"There's lots of kids out there who feel like they're nothing but dogs," said Anderson, referring to one of his favorite Bible verses, Ecclesiastes 9:4. "But if you're alive, if you're living, you have a future and you have a hope."

It's a message Harris was desperate to hear three years ago.

"It's like no matter how much money I had, or weed, or how much I partied, I was still empty. I was so empty," he said. Several times he contemplated suicide.

Anderson, who gave up his dream to become a dentist and has been working full time with young people for 10 years, said he has witnessed God's ability to impact people throughout the world.

"I'm involved because I've seen the change. I know what God can do in people's lives," he said. "I believe with all my heart that there's hope in God."

It's a belief he drives home week after week to the members of Legacy, Bethel's youth group. When Anderson first joined the church, there were eight teens in the group. Four years later, a typical Wednesday night youth service averages between 200 and 500 teens.

"I think what's significant about the work Scott Anderson and Bethel Church are doing is that they are reaching out to at-risk kids, gang kids, kids who really need the guidance the church is providing," said Redding police Capt. Steve Davidson, vice chairman of the Youth Violence Prevention Council.

Anderson joined the council's board of directors because he wants to break down walls between churches and the community, he said. He told conference-goers Thursday about some of the youth programs offered by area churches.

"There's lots of different things we can plug our kids into, and (churches) are just one of those, but I'm telling you, I've seen it work," Anderson said.

"I feel that what we have to say is important and what God has to offer will really touch lives," he said.

Lives such as Harris' and Bethel member Rich Potillor, a former Redding gang member who spoke at the conference about his life-altering encounter with God.

Scott Anderson, "I'm involved because I've seen the change. I know what God can do in people's lives. I believe with all my heart that there is hope in God."

It's with this passion that Scott brought the Love of Jesus week after week to Legacy, Bethel's youth group. Redding Police Captain Steve Davidson, speaks of Bethel's reaching out to at-risk kids, gang kids, and kids who really just need the guidance we should provide.

A community engaged, teenagers choosing Christ, an open heaven—that is the Transfer of Wealth!

SHIFT

PART TWO

REALIGNMENT: A GENERATIONAL ORDER

S tewardship is more than just handling money or overseeing a business. It is out of relationship that we honor the heart of the Master, including the fulfillment of His purpose.

In order for the Transfer to occur and provide a generational inheritance, there must be a realignment within the Bride of Christ. There is a Kingly (Governmental), anointing that has been displaced. With the restoration of Kings to the house of God and a reemergence of their mantel, a release in full measure will occur. Jesus said in John 12:32, "And if I be lifted up from the earth, I will draw all men unto Me."

**Transformation and dominion are
the outcome of this *Shift*.**

CHAPTER SIX

THE CONTAINER STORE ®

A PERSONAL FIT

Have you ever been in a Container Store®? Not only do they provide storage items, they also help structure a personal fit for your needs. Their focus is not exclusively on selling containers that store or hold your possessions, but teaching you how to use them in the best possible way for almost everything you need. They excel at elevating humanity through business known as Conscious Capitalism. Container Store managers and owners are consciously aware of their employees desires, as well as those of their customer base. What a great marketing example to follow!

Ever wonder about God's earthly storehouse? The Word says He has a bounty of wealth stored up for His children. I doubt God needs organizational help in heaven, although I believe He is consistently looking for suitable containers that can house His treasures here on earth. I am fully persuaded that the Lord seeks out human 'containers' that are capable of going the distance. Vessels that will carry and distribute what He would like to deposit in them. I think God may have invented Conscious Capitalism, as He is passionate about everyone! He desires to bring abundance to those He is building relationship with and trusts them to live in fulfillment, that others would be drawn to Him. Are you that 'container' God can store His treasure in? He owns it all, you know and for those who have been prepared for this moment in time, it is finally here. The expansion is coming quickly and you have been made ready for it.

VALUE OF THE VESSELS ... INSIDE OUT

Excitement and hope grows when you sense promotion is on the way. When the transfer of wealth occurs, it confirms that God has granted you influence and favor. After all, have not the people of God been toiling and praying for this very moment for a long time? Absolutely! His transfer of wealth and leverage is not just an assignment, but an honor. The Father is determinedly looking for more containers who can handle that kind of Holy substance.

Vessels are an important subject in the Bible and are addressed many times, revealing a pattern that should not be overlooked. In that pattern, God speaks a deliberate and significant message that He intends to have imprinted on our hearts. Take special notice and pay close attention to repetition, as it points to a truth that will make a genuine difference for your life. What we comprehend often influences what we embrace as value and can permanently determine the consequences, or benefits of our life choices.

We know a *Transfer* has been prophesied and we have been hearing about it for a long time. So why the delay? Perhaps it is due to a lack of available, ready vessels. Holy transfer of this magnitude cannot be put into just any container. In 2 Timothy 2:20-21, the disciple Timothy speaks of noble versus common jars, which can be identified *by their contents*. This scripture teaches that 'common' could become 'noble' by their own choosing. Yes, you read that correctly! If the content is the determining factor of the quality of my vessel, then what I choose plays a huge part in where He is able to use me. Perhaps it is time for some ordinary jars to *choose* to become extraordinary ones; choose wisely.

Jeremiah 2:11-13 speaks of the people of God who had changed what they valued and subsequently changed their 'glory.' They went from glorious to useless. What could be more sad? They gave greater worth to the things of their world, rather than their relationship to God. Thus, they became cisterns unworthy to hold His glory. A trait that is uniquely specific to the human race is that we have been given the ability to choose what consumes us. We can choose holy or unholy contents in our vessels.

Jesus' emphasis is always on the motives of your heart. Whatever truth we hold dear, determines our focus and ultimately our applied purposes in life. This is evident in Matthew 23:25-26 regarding the Pharisees and their roles. Jesus rebuked them for placing a greater importance on the outward appearance of the 'vessel' rather than what was on the inside. The Pharisees were not placed in the house of God to bring recognition to themselves, but to lead others to a more intimate relationship with the Father. However, in their self-promoting efforts they positioned themselves over the 'containers' who held no office. They created a perspective of His glory into something the Father never intended. The Pharisees had a role and a purpose to fulfill, but they turned it into a personal kingdom, not God's. They modeled someone holy on the *outside*, but *inside* they were full of death and iniquity.

> **Jesus' emphasis is always on the motives of your heart.**

Jesus' statement, "Clean the inside of the cup first" in verse 26, emphasized the greater importance of the unseen, where matters of the heart reflect the truth. The 'human' container should be full of the presence and glory of God, so its revealed in ways we may not comprehend. You may even find that a stable, although an unusual vessel, is perfectly suitable for the Son of God to reveal His glory. The Father's emphasis is not on grandeur, title or the external presentation.

Being born again and filled with His Spirit, does not guarantee that you are ready and available to contain the treasures He has appointed for transfer to this generation. You must value what God values. Your vessel must undergo preparation and you get to participate in the timing, the quality and the measure of His preparation. He so desires to engage with you, that He will withhold until you're willing to cooperate.

Let's evaluate the natural and the spiritual. Both natural and spiritual containers hold substance, however, each will hold a measured volume and when the contents exceed that limit, it will overflow. The spiritual realm measures value differently than the natural realm. In the Kingdom, we must remember that *being available and prepared is of great value to the Father's heart.*

All things laid equal, God is looking for a ready, accessible vessel to house His wealth, influence and favor; thus, enabling us to carry out His intentions during this *Shift*. You see, whoever is granted this great responsibility and honor, must realize that the promotions or influence that God may bring them had nothing to do with their credentials. It was always and only for the glory of God and his intended mission.

The pots used here, regardless of origin, must first be radiant with His love and secondly resemble the character of Jesus Christ. Like Jesus, his only objective was to reveal the Father's heart and take no glory for himself. The availability of the vessel, even in unfavorable condition, allows God to use and assign a new role. Bringing it home to where you live, no external 'qualifiers' such as status, education, lineage or achievement will earn what you desire. We are prepared on the Potter's wheel as God mold's us into a pliable and available vessel. The crafty hand of the Potter expands our capacity for love, relationship and resources, which He intends to spill over with effectiveness wherever we are placed.

VESSELS TO REVEAL HIS GLORY

David was a man after God's own heart. He didn't want to know about Him, he wanted to *know* Him. During his daily responsibilities, David found joy building relationship with the Father. He is an excellent example depicting intimacy with God. Moses did the same thing, although on the surface his journey looked much different than King David. David started in his father's field and ended up in the Father's palace. Moses started life in a borrowed palace, but ended up possessing all the land.

Moses, perhaps with an attitude, a temper and even impatient frustration, found a significant intimacy with God. In Exodus, Chapter 33, a noteworthy conversation takes place. Herein lies a secret to both David and Moses' affection with the living God. This passion, to experience an intimacy beyond anything they had known, is what drew the Father to reveal Himself in a tangible measure. Friendship with God is closer than a brother. Both men were entrusted with God's presence, His favor and His possessions. They became carriers of the glory of a God they loved and served.

In this conversation between God and Moses, the Father was frustrated with the people of Israel because of their disobedience and unfaithfulness to Him; not to mention a lack of appreciation and honor. God had just delivered Israel out of bondage in Egypt and established them as a people of His own choosing. He had been communing with Moses, laying the groundwork for the people to engage in relationship with Him.

Meanwhile, these chosen 'containers' were giving in to the selfishness of their flesh. Even in that moment, when the Father was overwhelmed with disappointment, angry at His own people, He kept His word. The verdict? God would send Israel into the promised land, but He would not accompany them. Instead, God told Moses He would send an Angel to go in His place. This decision froze Moses in his tracks!

Moses, after a forty-year jaunt in the desert, leads the Israelites out of bondage and through the Red Sea. He experiences forty intimate days with the Father up on the mountain. And now, in a desperation not to lose His presence, Moses cries out, *"Do not send us if you do not go with us"*. This man of God had experienced the person of God at such a deep level that, regardless of the benefits of a promised land, he was not going unless Father God went with him.

Moses wanted God, not His promises or benefits. The Father was Moses' reward! Wow, what a bondage-breaking, world-changing heart cry. Moses knew not only the importance of His presence, but knew what it was to walk in friendship with Him. He knew that without the Father intricately woven into the fabric of our daily life and journey, there could be no lasting pleasure or success.

The Father longs for those who want Him, and Him alone!

Here lies a readiness for transfer and God's *Shift*. His prosperity without His presence is a surefire disaster waiting to happen. The Father longs for those who just want Him. Not His power. Not His gifts. Not all the benefits He can provide. He longs for those who will sincerely love Him and Him alone.

At the core, the Father knew Moses' cry was a pivotal moment that qualified Israel's promotion into Canaan's land. They were going either way, but going with God's presence was a direct result of Moses' relationship to Him. You do not want the favor and blessing of the Lord without His radiant presence and glory in the center of it.

Remember, Moses would come down from the mountain glowing from God's Glory. He was not distracted by power or privilege. Moses eyes were only on the Father. He had discovered the secret place of intimacy and *that* was his priority. As a human container, although full of imperfections, Moses had been filled with the presence of his Father, his friend. This Moses could now be trusted with influence and position as a result of the interior heart changes the occurred from the palace to the desert.

David likewise loved God and lived for that relationship. Even during his lowest moments, David's heart cried out, "Don't take your Spirit from me". Everything else was an added benefit, but at David's core he simply wanted to know and experience this God he loved.

The unfolding story of the nation of Israel is an explanation of how God freely gave to them what they did not toil for (Deut. 6:10-12). It was Canaan's land, not Israel's, that God transferred to His children. Just like He did with Moses and the people of Israel, God wants to pour Himself and all that He is, into our generation. He intends to give us

Wealth transfer only occurs out of intimate, covenant relationship with God.

what we could not earn and release what has been stored up for us; Malachi 3:8-11.

This overflow comprised of wealth, favor and position, cannot be earned or acquired any other way except through intimate, covenantal relationship with Him. There was an investment in and between Moses and God that forged Moses into a vessel filled with the Lord's presence. The same preparation occurred with David, long before he was King. Remember, the container does not seek to reveal their own majesty, but merely reflect the Glory of God's.

DIRTY WATER WINE

The first recorded miracle in the life of Jesus, occurred at the Wedding feast in Cana. Late one night, as we were diving into the truth the Lord wanted to reveal, Deborah received a revelation from the Father about the details of this wedding feast. Being the creative God that He is, He chooses containers that man would typically never seek out for such an assignment. The story on the transformation of water into wine is impressive in its own right. However, the distinction of this miracle is about the type of containers that were chosen for the instant metamorphosis of water into heavens wine.

In John 2, when Jesus demonstrates himself in this first miracle, He was calculated with His actions. Theologians have overlooked the purposeful selection of the vessels that Jesus chose. These six, thirty-gallon pots, will forever be known on earth and in heaven for their greatest mission, revealing the Glory of the Son of God and not for the common, utilitarian cleansing pots they were made for.

Remember, Jews followed specific laws concerning what was sacred, especially for ceremonies. These laws were written with a focus on external compliance, as they interpreted God's law. Jewish law demanded that certain protocol must be adhered to. Unfortunately, these rituals often kept them from the Glory of God that was reserved for them.

Jesus was making a much larger statement in this first miracle. A miracle that speaks, yet today, for a generation awaiting the increase of His reign and the changes He will bring. The vessels selected by Jesus were the least likely containers ever to be used. *These containers had no sanctions through Jewish law or tradition for such purpose, much less deemed valuable by man.* Jesus' choice seemed contradictory in every way to Jewish procedures and sacred ceremonies.

These containers were stone pots that held approximately thirty to sixty gallons of water each. That is a lot of water! I doubt that they were moved much or cleaned very often, as these containers were normally used for ceremonial body cleansing, washing the dishes or even washing the feet of travelers. These utilitarian, ordinary vessels were chosen by Jesus to debut the Glory of His Father in miraculously turning of water into heaven's fine wine. According to Jewish law, dirty vessels were defiled; therefore, deemed unclean, and unable to be used for

Jesus chose the least likely vessels to debut His Father's Glory.

anything of sacred value. Can you imagine the shock to those who enjoyed the finest wine served, much less the host of the party, if they knew where the wine had come from in the first place? Dirty water made into high dollar wine! Dirty vessels made into clean containers. Now there is a novel idea.

In the exact moment Jesus commanded the water to change, He unveiled the true value of those containers. Their significance was not due to their glamorous form and refinement. No, Jesus prophetically blessed the containers, making what was unclean, instantly clean, both the pot and the water! Only after transformation could both the container and the contents reveal Jesus' purpose and bring His Father glory.

Why were they used, you ask? Simply because they were empty and available. Here is the kicker. God cleaned and filled those pots instantly and the ignoble became noble, by the Word of Jesus Christ.

Human vessels that are chosen to contain and overflow during this outpouring, perhaps did not start clean. Maybe they do not fit the traditions of man or the qualifications of some. However, the Father has already made provision for them. These containers have made themselves available to Jesus for His cause and for this unique time and transfer. Just like Jesus' first miracle, what God is doing now will not fit the mindset of our current religious paradigms. It will defy the traditions of man and if we are not careful, He will bypass many who are waiting to be ushered into the promotions of God's heart.

God does not qualify like man does. Will you support His chosen vessels?

I have heard numerous times from other spiritual leadership that God can use anything or anyone. Will they continue to promote that theology if God chooses those that earthly leaders may not deem an acceptable vessel? In Acts 10:15 it says, "Let no one call unclean what God has made clean". God will take the common and available and deem it noble. He will take the unclean and make it clean. And He begins right at home, inside of each one of us.

AN UNENDING SUPPLY

The kitchen is one of my favorite places. So much of life passes through it. Good conversation, mouth-watering aromas and a lifetime of memory-making events. Of all the rooms in any home, it probably has the most containers. Looking for a specific pot or bowl, I may find that it is already full of leftovers hiding in the refrigerator. Needing to find a container to hold what I need to save, I realize it's impossible for both the old and the new to occupy the same space. So, I must look through each one and recognize what needs to be emptied of its current contents in order to be used for what I need it to hold. You get the picture. Especially if you have ever opened up an old container of food buried in the back of the refrigerator, only to discover that the contents morphed into something other than their original form!

Once while speaking at a meeting in Florida, the Holy Spirit showed up as He often does. Those who attended that Sunday had an experience that made a permanent mark on their lives, especially me. I felt I was yielded to the Father, overflowing with His presence that day and was blessed that the Lord chose me. The mother of a dear friend of mine, whom I considered to be a hero in the Kingdom, came forward for prayer. Already surprised by her attendance, let alone her forward movement towards 'altar time', I was even more taken back when she spoke to me afterward. Following the service, she and her husband came to visit with me and in the course of that conversation she shared how moved and impacted she was by the Holy Spirit through my message. She assigned 90% of the impact she felt to 'my ability' and 10% was 'the Holy Spirit flowing through me.' She closed the conversation with, "Imagine how powerful the effect would have been if 10% was you and 90% was the Holy Spirit!" I was schooled, and I embraced what the Holy Spirit spoke to my spirit from her words. What a practical example for us to set as a standard. The next step in our preparedness to receive, is to search out what we must empty that could hinder us from receiving more of Him.

Scholarly studies have assigned Philippians 2:5-11 as the *Kenosis* passage, taking the interpretation from the Greek root word, to 'empty.'[1] According to this passage, Jesus emptied himself of all that was God to become human, qualifying as the only possible permanent sacrifice for sin. Jesus, who is 'The Christ', is our model. He became the only vessel His Father could use for this deliberate assignment. Like my example, we must empty ourselves for the Father to fill up and pour out.

In 2 Kings 4:3, Elisha the prophet directed the widow to go find all the empty vessels she had. God was establishing an unending supply of oil that the Holy Spirit would provide, not only for her, but her lineage as well. This is a developing pattern worthy of our attention. The Father is gathering every empty container to fill with the Oil of His Spirit for this present *Shift* and decreeing provision for an unending supply. He wishes to pour all that He is into those that are available; sharing His riches and revealing His glory through them.

Why did Jesus walk in so much authority, power, and resource? He didn't have posterity or wealth as men deemed it. Furthermore, there are examples of other Prophets and Kings that experienced similar lifestyles of authority noted in the Bible. Yet, the same life experience is infrequent in the typical Christian's life today. May I propose it is due to a principle I call "little is much?" We are, many times, so full of something other than God that there is no room for what really matters. Pat Robertson used the phrase, "An upside-down Kingdom"[2] once popular in Christian music lyrics. What we know as normal in the natural is often opposite to the way God chooses. God accomplishes fascinating works in ways we cannot comprehend and often using much less!

The Father does not want you to empty yourself from traits that make you unique; your personality, creativity and talents. However, without debate we should be filled with His nature and presence. The more we seek the life Jesus modeled, the more we will hunger for it. Having the mind of Christ and making room for the fullness of the Holy Spirit, produces an unending supply of His treasures. Our lives, God's container of choice, should be filled with His spiritual substance; love. Empty yourself of anything that displaces Him. When people experience the richness of His love through you, He will draw them to Himself.

THE HOLY CONTAINER, YOU!

In a simple spiritual equation, God chooses whom He chooses and His select vessel is you! The *Shift* has begun, but it had to begin in you first. This eye-popping demonstration of the greatest move of His Spirit, is coming through common, utilitarian pots. You and I may be nothing special in the eyes of our peers, but we have been prepared in secret for a very public display of His glory. *People without claim or reputation will lead this fresh outpouring of God.*

The greatest release of His glory will come through secretly prepared common pots!

These people, previously hidden, have been transparent and vulnerable to the Holy Spirit as He worked in the secret places of the heart. The Father is taking ordinary, common folk and filling them with His holiness as described in Isaiah 6:1-9. These realize they were unclean and unworthy, yet God sanctified them by taking the coals of fire to their lips, purging anything that does not resonate with His Holy kiss and commanding them to go into all the world!

The making of "holiness" is not reduced to just the removal of sinful behavior. This involves the preparation of the heart and mind to be transformed in Him, a three-chorded strand that cannot be broken. The Lord is filling vessels with Himself in untold measures. The presence of God was never intended to be contained within man-made buildings. A massive expansion of the Kingdom has started throughout and being carried out by common containers full of His love and His presence.

The resources stored up are meant for invasion and territorial takeover for His Kingdom. He is okay if you become wealthy, because you cannot be bought. However, some perceive it's for a personal Canaan land inheritance; that's secondary. His resources are not intended for selfish gain. They are to be used to fulfill the needs of others, take care of the poor, take over the places where darkness holds dominion and always to display His love toward us.

The containers in this unique transfer, can only be satisfied with more of Jesus, not what He gives.

This new demonstration of God's glory will be found in Holy vessels maintaining relationship with Him as their Father and friend first and foremost, rather than His benefits. Like David and Moses, to live in relationship with the person of God is greater than any inheritance He has promised and will fulfill in you. Psalms 42:1 says, "As the deer pants for the water so my soul pants for you" (NIV). This is a picture of indescribable thirst that can only be quenched by one thing; the living water of God. As deer can only be satisfied with water, so they, who are used in this unique transfer of wealth, can only be satisfied with more of Jesus.

OVERFLOWING CONTAINERS

As we discovered earlier in this chapter, it is what is on the inside that really matters. An eloquent or expensive container is great, but if the contents are not worth drinking when offered to others, it will not be accepted. In John Chapter 4, the story of the Woman at the Well was about water and thirsting for it. She soon realized that she was thirsty for more than water from a well. She was thirsting for the living water; Jesus.

There is an interesting parallel between the discussion in this passage on living water and the word used for the baptism of the Holy Spirit. The word for baptism here is the Greek word 'baptisma' and it describes infilling and saturation.[3] Much like a piece of wood that has been left in the water for a long period of time that it became saturated to the point of being waterlogged, so was this woman.

You can become so 'soaked' with the natural things in life that there is not much room for Holy deposits. God is not stingy. He has much to give back and Jesus will distribute His treasures in the right order and in the right seasons of your life.

Drinking from the living water Jesus has to offer fills you to a level *of intoxication.* This my friend, you want to experience! This is not just being saturated with Him, but super-saturated so much so that you leak everywhere you go. In Luke 2, Jesus increased in favor with both God and man. Favor is a product of your intimacy with God. When your time with Him supersaturates your life, it will spill out of you and into the places you live. Jesus never lacked because he lived out of His Father's supply; the Provider and Giver of all things. His number one priority was spending time deepening His relationship with His Father and then walking in obedience of it.

He declared more than once, as I paraphrase John 5:19, "I only say what I hear the Father saying and I only do what I see the Father doing." Thus, His example for us is to do the same.

In 2 Timothy 2:20-21, Paul speaks of both noble and common vessels. A common container can be used for noble purposes *if* its available to pay the price. The Father is assigning places for you to go, occupy and carry heaven's influence. Will you consider your choices holy choices so He can transform lives and answer the cry of society? His focus is on the contents inside the container; the emptying of you and availability to Him. Now you have His attention.

Drink from the Living water and become intoxicated with His presence!

CHAPTER SEVEN

STEWARDING THE SHIFT

A DRAMATIC WAKE-UP CALL

In 1998, four days before the Thanksgiving holiday, I received an unusual phone call. A well-known movie producer in the industry called to inquire if I was available to fly out the day after Thanksgiving and meet with this Hollywood icon. Of course, I immediately said yes! A flood of emotion and a myriad of thoughts raced through my mind. What a great opportunity this would be. For starters, it was just plain exciting as it brought back memories of my Grandfather and the realms of Hollywood he worked with and I was exposed to as a young man. Then I realized this may be an opportunity to affect someone of great magnitude and influence them for the Kingdom of God.

Furthermore, this could overflow and seriously impact the entertainment industry. I rallied my network of intercessors to begin to pray for God's intervention and arranged my flight. Two days later, the day before Thanksgiving, I received a second call from the same individual. "I am sorry Dr. Larson, due to a schedule change we have to cancel your appointment," he said. At one level I felt relieved, and yet on another very disappointed.

Later that night I was awakened by the Lord speaking to my heart. He said, "I canceled the meeting." I pressed in for about an hour asking why. His response to me came early Thanksgiving morning and it rocked my world! The Lord said to me that until I learned how to handle the influence that such an open door would present, He would not permit me to do so, as it would lead to roads I was not prepared to travel upon and possibly derail me from the path He had in store.

A transfer of wealth and/or influence beyond my current level of experience, required a major heart preparation for my ability to properly and successfully steward it. The Lord was not punishing me by closing those doors. Rather, it was more like extended credit; a future glimpse into my destiny that God said was waiting for me to enter into.

This container needed some further reinforcement and internal conditioning. God creates situations for us wherewith we release life and healing. Even though the phone call came through a trusted relationship, that directional *Shift* of influence may have delayed the fine tuning I needed.

In Hebrews 4:12 the Bible speaks of His word being sharper than any two-edged sword. Further down in the same passage, it speaks more specifically about discerning the motives of the heart. These motives link directly to personal prosperity and success. What the Lord revealed to me about the mantle of influence was shocking. The Holy Spirit clearly said to me, "I would open more doors for my people if they would not use my favor for personal promotion." He is a jealous God and He does not share His glory.

This is no different. How many times has a Christ follower impacted someone of notoriety, only then to plaster the story all over the Internet and use that event to raise money or validate themselves and their career? That does not even come close to stewardship, humility or discretion and the Father will not open doors of lasting wealth and impact unless His principles are tattooed on our hearts.

DEFINING ROLES

Stewardship is a concept frequently discussed, but requires a closer look. The word "steward" in a Biblical sense is far removed from the word used in our culture. In a truer sense, it is disappearing from common use altogether as the Father is growing and reproducing sons. Nonetheless, a steward was a servant in a master's household or one assigned to a position overseeing a business. There were servants and then there were heads over servants, thus the need for *a steward*. Those servants were trustworthy and had earned a full measure of the Master's confidence in them. Loyalty was high on their character list of values.

Key components in Biblical description brings clarity to this role. This helps us secure a greater understanding of our roles as 'stewards' in the Kingdom of God. A steward did not own the possession he supervised or cared for. His or her responsibility was to see to their Masters' success and bring increase to the endeavor assigned to them. At the end of the day, they were servants with unique positions and privileges. In Genesis, Chapter 15, the Biblical narrative regarding Abraham's chief steward, or senior servant, where Abraham states that Eliezer would inherit all of his possessions if he did not have a natural born heir. Already we can see there is a deeper, more familial and intimate relationship with a steward than with a servant. This is why the master was so disappointed when the steward did not follow through with expectations given in Luke 19:11-13 regarding the Parable of the Talents. Reread that passage again with a more intimate understanding of the relationship between master and steward. The steward had greater privileges, greater responsibilities and experiences, thus a higher expectation of obedience to execute on behalf of the master. It brings a clear insight to the responsibility of one entrusted with his master's wealth. Remember, our heavenly Father is the Master and we are His Steward and a son or daughter.

IN THE BEGINNING

Genesis 1:27-31 records a permanent role of assignment given to man to steward God's possession, the earth.

> *27 So God created mankind in his own image, in the image of God he created them; male and female he created them. 28 God blessed them and said to them, "Be fruitful and increase in number; fill the earth and subdue it. Rule over the fish in the sea and the birds in the sky and over every living creature that moves on the ground." 29 Then God said, "I give you every seed-bearing plant on the face of the whole earth and every tree that has fruit with seed in it. They will be yours for food. 30 And to all the beasts of the earth and all the birds in the sky and all the creatures that move along the ground—everything that has the breath of life in it—I give every green plant for food." And it was so. 31 God saw all that he had made, and it was very good. And there was evening, and there was morning—the sixth day. (NIV)*

So, in basic form, the earth is the Lord's and He has instructed us to subdue and manage it for Him. As referenced earlier, Arthur

Burke calls it the "Garden Mandate." That plan, from the beginning, still remains. However, after the cross and the infilling of the Spirit, this stewardship role takes on an expanded definition and much larger parameters as it now includes a spiritual dimension.

STEWARDSHIP VS. OWNERSHIP

God set the mandate in the book of Genesis. Jesus brings clarity throughout His teachings in the New Testament, by setting a foundation and establishing the reality that we are stewards, not owners, of God's possessions. He wants to change our inward perspective. All of creation is the Fathers!

A few weeks into writing this book, Deborah and I had the pleasure of meeting a gentleman who has been given a remarkable ability to discover, through the wisdom of God, where subterranean natural resources can be found. I must admit when we first sat down to visit with him, it was a bit unbelievable. In fact, the things discussed were so far-fetched that I relied on my prophetic wife, who was seated next to him, to bring a confirming word.

There is no lack in heaven. Yet we worry about enough? There is nothing God has not thought of or missed during any season of challenge.

Accessing the creativity of heaven to discover treasures hidden in the earth is an example of what the Father is ready to release upon his children. However, the most remarkable impression we took away with us was that his mild-mannered attitude was in line with the King's. In his own words, "It's all God's. If He wants to, He just makes more." There is no lack in heaven. Yet we worry about enough? There is nothing God has not thought of or missed during any season of challenge.

It is noteworthy that this man lives a simple, balanced lifestyle. He is willing to partner with anyone God aligns him with, so at just the right time, we can tap into whatever resource the Father has stored for us. This man does not look to gain wealth for himself. Instead, he operates a nonprofit ministry to meet the needs of orphans overseas. His attitude about the powerful and valuable gift he has been given is pure; "It is the Father's and He will use it however He chooses to. My role is to listen, act, and obey."

Like some of you, we too have unknowingly aligned ourselves with wrong partners. We have tried to help God get things done. In a moment of impatience, or even out of natural wisdom, we make decisions with those we thought we were equally yoked with, only to find out that their intentions and focus were in a much different place. Those decisions were costly.

That is what happened to this man. Some so-called spiritual leaders exploited his gift and purity of heart then used his gift to profit themselves, experiencing a substantial increase to their personal net worth. The Kingdom of God is never advanced with this attitude. Apparently, the heart of stewardship quickly morphed into one of personal gain; ownership. The mandate God had given them was lost. When discussing this with our friend, his heart rang true as he replied, "God will deal with them, as that is not my concern. Remember it is all His anyway." This is the heart of a true steward! He is accomplishing what God has called him to do for the Kingdom and in obedience to his Father. He is not famous or rich and rejects the limelight, maintaining a demeanor that loudly declares, "Everything is God's and I am a steward, not an owner." He is part of God's unified army set out to influence the world God's way!

Western mindsets continue to oppose the most important attitude in our current *Shift*. More than once, Jesus talked about how we are to be faithful with little in order to be trusted with more. Do you think He was speaking about an ability to balance a budget of ten thousand dollars vs. ten billion dollars? I don't. I believe it is in reference to molding one's character so as not to lay claim to all that God has provided, for and through you.

Dave Ramsey, a national radio host discusses personal finance from a Biblical view. I respect his stand regarding attitudes and perspectives about money; providing balanced systems which produce self-control, a fruit of the Spirit. Too many followers of Christ are deeply in debt and poorly stewarding what has been entrusted to them thus far. How can they be responsible for more of God's treasures when so many internal perspectives need changing?

Stewardship is not just about money. It involves spiritual gifts, the favor of the Lord, and positions of influence. How do we handle those? Do we use what was given to us for personal increase and identity? Do we manipulate situations with the favor of God and throw out the 'Jesus card' like a free pass to tilt the scale on our behalf? Many have adulterated the Lords reputation because of their internal need for personal gain and recognition.

Like the parable of talents found in Matthew 25:14-30, the Father gives each a talent or two to begin with. We can choose to bury them, gamble them for a potential gain, or spend them on hope for greater identity by collecting things that man values as wealth. We must place a greater value on His possession because we hurt the reputation of Christ and impede the advancement of the Kingdom when operating in the fashion just described above.

Remember, internal values are forged out of intimate relationship, and that produces a proper understanding of the great responsibility and privilege He has given us. Stewardship comes with a higher expectation to produce increase and bring it back to Him, whom we love so much. Herein, we defend the honor of the Master. This code must be entwined in our hearts. If it is, it will provide clear insight on why we are entrusted with the Master's wealth to manage from the natural roles He has placed us in and thrive.

GOD'S INTELLECTUAL PROPERTIES

Recently creative ideas have been a large part our business and ministry development. We found that if you want to learn about the values of God and the character in men, just talk to someone about the 'ownership' of their business and listen closely to what they say. Wisdom sets a precedence to carefully steward every project and idea with an understanding of who it belongs to. Take note as the tendency to grip tightly is very common, even among professing Christian entrepreneurs.

In working with entrepreneurs, discussions about intellectual property (IP) is common. Creative entrepreneurs are very concerned about retaining 'ownership' of their IP when looking into recruiting investment funds. Intellectual property is a very 'rich' investment and can yield ginormous dividends. When an idea is being ripened, the originator of the idea should rightfully claim the IP and be compensated accordingly. A movie called, *The Social Network*, was devoted to the issue of dealing with Intellectual Properties concerning the internet platform commonly known as Facebook. If you do not think IP is important, just watch the movie. It will give you a broader view of the value of creativity;

especially if it comes from above! If you want to experience serious drama, get into an IP battle. Stay with me here. We are fully aware that there are interlopers who steal ideas, rob inheritances and will happily stake claim to what has been given to you. The details of all that are perhaps for another book.

However, unrelated to outright thieves, there remains an underlying poverty mindset that has poisoned the relationship many have with the Father. When operating from a poverty-driven perspective, we give legal access for the devourer to deceive, steal and destroy what is rightfully given to us. This is all the more reason that we must break off any mindset that is not rooted in Him. We must choose rightly, staying consistent with His heartbeat.

I am fully persuaded that the Father is releasing an unprecedented flow of available resources and influence for His children, so we can take action like the Kings we are created to be. The body of Christ should be leading in all facets of culture so what we do impacts all around us and fosters change. It's not hard to understand that heavens creativity started with Him in Genesis 1:1 where he demonstrated the greatest creative acts for the first time.

There is a transfer in motion and it's time to get in the current of where He is taking it. Those with non-negotiable values written upon their hearts, that everything they do should reproduce for His Kingdom. Every idea for business, arts, entertainment, provision or any advancement are solely God's Intellectual Property and when we develop and implement His IP for His intended purpose, He shares in the bounty! We are sons and daughters of the Father and co-labor for His purpose and, just like King David, He will bless His own very well.

George Washington Carver was once a slave, then became a free man and subsequently one of America's greatest entrepreneurs. He

It's God's Intellectual Property. When we develop it for His purpose, He shares in the bounty!

was a man of great faith. Read about his discovery of peanuts and the multitude of uses he found in them. In doing so, you will understand how he received his ideas and who received the credit; for it's a God IP. In this current vacuum of economic and social unrest, God is giving His people problem-solving ideas and long-term strategies for all aspects of life. When He releases an idea, I believe He expects good use of it with an assumed increase and proper credit given. Biblical principles support the Law of Increase that will operate in your life, which precipitates yet even more trust and creativity as you demonstrate to Him, through the works of the Holy Spirit, the fruit of your labor.

Do you want to be a transforming activist in God's *Shift* and find He arranged for you to receive from the Holy Spirit new creative ideas, sounds, solutions, problem-solving wisdom, and life-sustaining inventions? Then determine the answers to these fundamental questions within your heart. Who owns it? Who receives the glory? What do you do with the financial increase to benefit the Master's purpose? If you answer these in tandem with His heart, you will be well-dressed for a *Shift* and transfer currently underway.

LOOSEN YOUR GRIP!

When unsettling times come, people choose whether to embrace faith or fear. You may think not, or you may battle through, but it's always your choice. Observing behavior under pressure, often people default to what they know; gripping tightly to what little they have. This poverty mindset is self-defeating, self-perpetuating, and usually a generational influence. Extreme cases have been televised showing people hoarding trash, newspapers, clothes, food and really just about anything. Hoarders are fear-driven and fear can suffocate you. It can dominate thoughts and actions, and paralyze you from moving forward.

Extreme fears like claustrophobia and acrophobia, or extreme fear of heights, are examples of this. Fear plays upon and releases all the untransformed thoughts and emotions within us. Fear creates agreement with the lies of the enemy and agreements of any kind empower Him to work harder against us. The more effective response is to grab on to faith and cling to the Faith Giver. The result is freedom! When the Father removes the root of fear, He exchanges it with His peace and that releases joy, laughter, rest and provision, then His placement will abound.

I am aware that my words can flow easily and at times may leave you wondering, "Do these people have any idea what I am really going through? Have they ever walked the road I have been down"? May we share with deep, honest emotion? Yes! Did you read the first sections of this book? We have, and continue to walk in, the same footsteps you do, just different battles and growth. Behind every word we write, there is another story like yours.

Deborah is a woman of great faith, valor and heart. There seems to be nothing she would not entrust to the Father and she certainly does not have a poverty mindset. Although she is the strongest person I have ever known, when she told Him she would go the distance, she had no idea what that road would look like. From childhood, her journey required a daily dependence on someone else providing, which proved most challenging, especially with her God-given talents and resources. Like many of us, she struggled with self-sufficiency, trusting that God would do exactly what He promised. He most certainly will keep His promise through an avenue that stretches you into stronger, more resilient faith, but He will do it!

This is something that everyone faces at one time or another. When you have been trained on the path of self-sufficiency and count on your efforts for financial supply, it can be very difficult depending solely on God. So, when He asks you to lay down your own abilities and let Him be your source, it can trigger a collision between the natural and the spiritual. Such a request contradicts the very principles that you may have lived from. However, when miraculous events come after the trial has passed, it's easy to share the testimony. It's during the *daily* adventure that lasting victory is won. Most know in their head that He does not lack, but when you trust him with everything, both natural and spiritual, you will apprehend an abundant surplus.

During the early years of our journey together, we were not allowed to share our needs with others. This wasn't an easy task and proved to be a lonely one. We solicited no prophetic words, but when they came, they were timely and accurate. It was not that God did not provide, or that we had mindsets that prohibited His release; no. It was time for the Lord to develop deeper level of trust, dependency and relationship. He has called both of us to step out of the boat and walk to Him on the water in obedience to His request.

Some days Deborah would do everything she was asked and still not get breakthrough for weeks or months. Other days were spent soaring with wings of eagles, walking in the High Places of His Kingdom. Knowing God has entrusted us with great favor, prepared for this *Shift,* we sport a stronger confidence! Even through moments when He allows us to grow through the guttural issues of life, like the recent loss of her son, Jeremy Stoke, the fire inspector who died in the recent CARR fire in Redding, CA. He keeps His promises to us and likewise, will keep them to you.

Our Father is faithful to walk with you through everything. Proverbs 11:24 states, "One person gives freely, yet gains even more; another withholds unduly, but comes to poverty." Thus, a mentality of anything less than knowing He is for you and demonstrating it with a generous heart, will hinder the work of God and is a strong sign that Mammon has touched your life. We found that it's His mercy that He would take us through the growth times so we can succeed, for there is power in the process.

How do you know if you struggle with self-reliance, greed, or fear of lack? Reflect on your attitudes and actions regarding money. Look at your bank statements. Where do you spend it? Where we place our money reveals the 'values' we hold. Consider your generosity meter. When God gives you something, do you grip tightly or look for ways to bring increase and bless the Lord with a joyful spirit? My friend, who is able to locate natural resources, says it best, "It is all God's." I asked him about the dwindling oil and natural gas supply and he chuckled as he answered, "That's man's problem with fear. God just creates more!" That simple response capsulated the whole discussion down to core issues: God's creativity and man's fear! You will never abound with His blessing if fear and control are prevalent in you. Freely you have received, freely give. Loosen your grip and embrace trust; He is for you!

GOOD STEWARDSHIP DEFINED

In Genesis Chapter 24, regarding the story of Abraham and the role of his chief servant, the steward, we discover the behaviors of a well-defined steward. According to this passage, a good steward demonstrates these characteristics:

1. **A good steward listens carefully to the Master's instruction.** Abraham gives very detailed instructions on where to find a wife for his son and how to bring her back and he obeys.

2. **A good steward is totally devoted to the purpose or task assigned by his master.** Abraham had the steward swear allegiance to the plan and the steward honored his commitment by his actions, not his words.

3. **A good steward carefully executes the master's instructions.** He did exactly as he was instructed.

4. **A good steward delivers the expected results!** The servant returned with the bride that Isaac needed.

5. **A good steward seeks wisdom from the Father, and power from on high.** In his journey, the steward stayed the course. When he needed help, he inquired of the Lord: "God of my master Abraham, make me successful today." This was the fulfillment of James 1:5, even before it was written: "If any of you lack wisdom, let him ask of God, that giveth to all men liberally, and upbraideth not; and it shall be given him." Supernatural power and wisdom was made available to complete the God-ordained task.

6. **A good steward operates out of abundance.** The steward was generous as his master was generous. There was no lack! He brings fine gifts on a camel to the Father of Isaac's future bride. The master made provision for what was necessary to fulfill the contract for a bride.

7. **A good steward carries out his assignment with full authority and favor.**

The Lord trains His stewards well. They know to enter every situation with authority and position with a humble heart ready to fulfill the master's mandate. He is in charge. Like Jesus, when the locals tried to throw Him off a cliff, Jesus simply walked through their midst with authority, poise and peace, escaping unharmed.

The Lord has assigned Deborah and I to function not as pastor's in the marketplace, but as entrepreneurs living in His favor. He intends that we not only succeed in business, but we do so with integrity and valor. We also function as a Priest whether we are leading our Community of believers on a given Sunday, or He creates opportunity through our business relationships. To minister in the financial world, where He has directed our influence to be, our reputation must precede us. Long before meeting with successful and influential individuals, they have already googled information on us or sought out to discover who we are and how we operate. Our character opens the door for direct representation

Character opens the door to abundance as you represent Christ in every decision.

of the Christ. During the course of a conversation, we are often asked about what motivates our choices. Our most common response is that we answer to One that is higher than natural authority. Deborah eagerly shares about her relationship with Jesus and how He directs our decisions and actions. He shows us how to consummate deals others may fail at because of the creative strategies He gives both of us.

We've been in various situations where others tried to complete a transaction that seemingly would not come together; but then the Lord delivers it like a package. Once, we entered a business deal late in the transaction; virtually unknown to the principles. Within days, a financial transaction was in motion. Those leaders struggled with that transaction for over a year. One of the businessmen wrote an email thanking us for the development and crediting Deborah and I with the success. Deborah, in her unique way to share the Gospel said, "Thank you, but it's the Fathers delight and His favor over our lives that brought the results." She moves so naturally with Jesus in business circles that most know Jesus is a significant partner in our life. No one has voiced disapproval, they are just aware He is a part of all we do. When the whole of your life integrates Christ, the opportunities for people to inquire about Him are right in front of you. We find people struggle with so-called, 'witnessing' because the Kingdom is outside of their professional and sometimes personal activities. It's easy to discuss the greatest thing in your life, when He is woven into every realm you live in; natural and supernatural.

The *Shift* becomes evident when we live-out-loud, bringing Jesus into every conversation as a friend, mentor, partner and our spiritual coach! Not only is it easier to share His love with others, but give Him the glory in all the transactions He brings your way. That *Shift* in you, will release greater power to transact all His well-laid plans. Today is an opportunity for the internal *Shift* integrating Jesus in every facet of your life!

Recall the Hebrew perspective; they are "God-centered" and everything in their life flows out of His hand, thus, He is a part of the transaction and the outcome. This will change our society as we grow in the favor and posterity of the Lord. That lifestyle draws the affection of heaven, the attention of the Father validating you as His chosen are trusted with His plans.

Jesus confirms this in His parable about Stewardship. Matthew 25:14 says, "Again, it will be like a man going on a journey, who called his servants and entrusted his wealth to them." Jesus makes reoccurring declarations such as, "Who then is a faithful and wise steward?" or, "He who is faithful in little will be given much." Some among us have reduced Jesus words to mean spiritual gifts and prosperity, when in context, Jesus clearly spoke of the character of one who can be trusted to take authority over everything that is His Father's. How much God trusts you to represent Him, which lends to greater release for more, is truly up to you.

SHIFT HAPPENS, NOW WHAT?

I have stated enthusiastically that the transfer of wealth and the treasures of heaven's storehouse have been appointed to this generation. Now what do we do with it? The undeniable principle of good stewardship, as taught by Jesus himself, comes into effect.

So, what *would* you do with an increase of resources and influence? Will you build a bigger house, write a book, appear noble and throw money at relationships in need, or blog about it on your website? Although none of these activities individually are poor choices, it really all depends on what He has told you to do. If you are not listening for God's direct assignments and strategies, it can and will be squandered. God will not fund ideas that will lead to your demise, and even success can separate you from His purpose if you are not ready for it. Our heart and more importantly our character must be ready for promotion. To advance the Kingdom, we must position ourselves according to the Spirit as He decides who, what, where, when and how.

Are you Ready? God will not fund anything that will separate you from His purpose.

Like Mr. Carver, would you maximize His creativity and develop multiple streams of increase? What if God gave you a military strategy that far exceeded anything before, to defeat any enemy?

Are you ready for that level of trust and influence? Well, God did that for both Gideon and King David. It is not outside of Him to do it here and now as well. With God's downloaded ideas comes favor with man and remarkable amounts of wealth and resources. In that culture, Israelites were known for their gold earrings and various adornments. Much of that gold was collected from the spoils of battle. Talk about sudden, unexpected wealth.

What would you do if others saw your success and sought out your advice and influence? Perhaps the President of the United States sought your help with an economic solution. What would you do? However, you answer such questions will reveal if you are ready to occupy this *Shift*. In all honesty, admitting you do not know what you would do except seek the heart of the Father, is the best answer. Most likely, the advancement of your role in this transfer will not be that sudden or overwhelming and more likely come steadily and measurably. But, it could just happen overnight as in the day of Gideon's victory.

When the *Shift* occurs, it often feels like a 'suddenly' moment, though you and I know it was in the making for many years. In that moment, as you experience the overwhelming emotion of gratefulness, humility and even shock, remember, it is all about Jesus. Bow before Him and give honor where it is due.

The following helps guide your daily application to hearing the direction God wants you to take next:

1. Stay close to the Father's heart and maintain your intimate time with Him. It is more essential now than ever before.

2. Listen attentively to God's instructions and strategies. When He speaks, write it down. Take all of the prophecies you have kept, or pondered

over and review them. Ask the hard questions and do not move until released to do so.

3. Proclaim His increased favor over your life to speak and influence others with the message of Jesus Christ. Look for open doors and listen for His leading. As Deborah would say, Posture yourself for Promotion.

4. Shut your ears to the voice of the enemy, no matter who's mouth it comes out of! Do not lend your ear to every 'out of the woodwork' need. Everyone has them and you are not God. You act only upon His direction. God is their provider, just as He is yours. Remember that.

5. Be wise with money choices whether great or small. Stewards always produce an increase. If the opportunity does not show increase, it may not be a God one.

6. Be generous, for God's generosity should operate through you. Giving out of empathy is not of the Father! Giving out of compassion bathed in love will come from the whispers of His heart to yours. Then you will know with overwhelming urgency and passion to move with His every directive.

7. Follow the simple admonition: "Whether in word or deed, do it all to the glory of God."

Two things mark a successful spiritual life, as Paul repeats in many of his introductions; "That Christians would be known for their faith toward God and love for the saints." The question is not whether the *Shift* is in motion, but at what level you will participate and with what mindset. I speak over you increase, favor, boldness and a love for God and for His people.

CHAPTER EIGHT

FINANCED TO OCCUPY

I t has been established in previous chapters that a major *Shift* is in process and it will permanently change the role and position of the Body of Christ if they choose it. It's meant to bring an upward swing to our economy and our culture. Although we have ups and downs in our culture, this is different. You can be assured there will be no casual disbursement of His abundance; financial or influence. His timing is perfect. Like a set of tumblers that need to fall in specific order to open a lock, the right combination of events have linked. Everything has been strategically positioned to unlock the mystery of God's plans. As the final tumbler moves into place, we will see the unveiling of the Father's strategy for our generation and those to come.

HIS NATION OCCUPY 'TIL I COME

1 Peter 2:9 describes a chosen group of Royal descent, known as a "Holy Nation," that reveals the very nature and character of a Sovereign God. As a people group under the direction of Heaven's government, we should be identified by attributes of our 'native' land. When we meet someone from another country

we can immediately identify a foreigner by their accent. However, you may notice that although they speak the same language, their behavior and their traditions are also different from your culture. This is true no matter what country you are from! Thus, the Father identifies us by qualities He would like represented by His citizens. A Holy and chosen tribe, displaying the likeness or the 'character' of His son, Jesus. No matter where we reside, we are expected to influence this world with His culture. He calls that 'occupying'. This is where one of Jesus' comments stands out appropriately. In Luke 19:11-13, Jesus shares the *Parable of Talents* relating it directly to Heavens Kingdom. He closes the discourse on the resources he gave them with a command to, "Occupy 'til I come."

> **To occupy means setting up tents to live in, and amongst a foreign land.**

So, what exactly did He mean by occupy? The word 'occupy' means to be in residence, to establish or permeate.[1] The Lord expects His Bride to embed themselves within their culture. Further, 'to occupy' means to set up tents in order to live in and amongst them. It speaks of engaging in transactions, relationships, becoming involved in government, school district, and various areas within the city or region that you live in. That's what foreigners do when they leave their native land, traveling off to another country. They must 'occupy' to become acquainted with and participate in their chosen land. This does not mean they embrace the identity of the new land, but simply establish themselves there and make a difference. So is it in the Kingdom of Heaven. Jesus, as the son of God, thought it not robbery to be equal with man, and He humbled himself, serving others in and amongst the people, Philippians 2:6-8 (paraphrased). At the same time, He reflected the culture of Heaven with the character of His Father. We as the Body of Christ, must do the same. And how will they know that we are citizens from another land? John 13:34-35 states, "A new commandment I give you: Love one another. As I have loved you, so also you must love one another. By this all men will know that you are My disciples, if you love one another." Love is both the dialect and currency of Heaven.

Once Christ has embedded you in your sphere(s) of influence, you are positioned to affect the region He has given you to dominate. For you to 'occupy' with the fragrance of Heaven, you must lead with Love. No matter what region He places you in, you cannot occupy and bring Heaven's government here on the earth without Love. Then, when love is predominant in all aspects of your life, the *Shift* will occur. Heaven's approval, power, and opportunities will expand right where He planted you! That has been His plan from the beginning.

Although some may travel globally and others may be positioned to rise up from a local to national influence, there will always remain an effective impact in every local region. Sometimes we lose focus, looking down the road for the next, larger assignment. But God has set you in a region necessary for you to carry His government and authority to bring dramatic change.

The *Shift* must begin right where you are, not where you are going. From a Hebrew perspective, taking an aerial view of His plan makes perfect sense. Jesus says, "Stay here and finish the work I have started; begin with love. If love is a currency, then when you trade criticism or judgment for love, Heaven will open like a portal and provide legal admittance into every area of our culture. Then you will 'occupy' right where you are and He will pour out all the treasures He's stored to finance where He will take you next. You can expect the wealth of His glory to bring people and opportunities to you." Transformation will be a natural outcome.

What does this have to do with the wealth and stature God wants to give the church? From my first stint with an open heaven, I know this for sure; where God guides He provides. He is not in the business of randomly disbursing anything, and He won't distribute natural resources if love has not opened the door. The heavens will open and pour out upon what, and who He is blessing. Our focus should be bringing all things, rightfully God's, into order with His government. Our lives, our families, our businesses and the communities we live in can come under the statues of heaven through us and be *transformed.* Now that is an occupation worth spending your life for.

NATION, TRIBE, AND FAMILY

From the onset, God's people have been set up to experience nothing but success. His *nation***,** the "Children of God," includes everyone who embraced Jesus Christ as the redemption for their sin and made him Lord of their lives. He further divides His nation into smaller groups called *tribes*. In the Old Testament, these tribes were unique family groups. For example, each one of the twelve sons of Jacob became a distinct tribe. They functioned with specific traits, setting them apart from one another. In 1 Chronicles 12, King David's army identifies many of the characteristics that set them apart from one another. The Tribe of Levi was charged with the responsibility of Priest. The Tribe of Judah is known as the Tribe of Kings, and the most preeminent of the 12 tribes. The Tribe of Benjamin was known for the archer's ambidextrous ability to sling stones & shoot arrows. The Tribe of Gad were experts with shield and spear and swift as gazelles on the mountains. The characteristics were for purpose and when brought together, created a force to be reckoned with; God's chosen people. Today in the Kingdom of God, there is little identifiable evidence of a tribal family. However, be it ministry, business or a societal movement, technically we are still a tribe.

Seth Godin, author and entrepreneur, describes a 'tribe' as a focus group or one's niche market.[2] Conversely, as others can affect our thinking and doing, we as the 'Tribe' or Body of Christ are capable of making a tremendous impact. Remember each Tribe of Israel had specific responsibilities, and today, although dispersed throughout many regions, we are no different!

The next division is that of a *family*. That's easier to grasp. It is a literal family unit. The Bible says first the natural, then the supernatural. There are families with natural DNA and families with supernatural, or spiritual DNA. Deborah and I are a physical family, but we were a spiritual family first. How we see the Kingdom of God and view life is like we were born from the same parents. We were very much alike in the spirit before a choice of marriage became an option.

We now give birth to spiritual sons and daughters and our Kingdom offspring share a passion for both the development of Kings and Priests. A 'Spiritual parent' should focus on those they have led to

True transfer must be generational.

Christ and teach them accordingly. You see, true transfer must be generational, whereby it carries on long after you finish your race. Do a checkup from the neck up. Who discipled you? Who are you discipling? God's family is made up of individuals where growth and transfer naturally occurs.

HIS PLAN ... INDIVIDUALLY

The power of one is often overlooked. Although it has been a strong building block for many network marketing businesses, it was originally the foundation of the church in the New Testament. Jesus was the original 'one.' Nothing is more powerful than one person making a difference for another. The Lord made a difference for each of us and He has not forgotten that we need His continual guidance and impartation. This is a very personal journey and although God is globally focused, He has not forgotten you.

In Psalms, Chapter 139, the Father addresses your individuality, personality, physical characteristics, giftings and choices. All throughout the Word, He brings everything down to 'one.' That 'one' is you. From the Song of Solomon, with the kisses from God's lips, clear through the guidance of Paul in Romans, Chapter 8, where Paul addresses condemnation and sin. This entire journey with Christ is all about you. Thus, the transfer of all of His Kingdom begins with you.

> **"A man's heart devises his way: but the Lord directs his steps."**
>
> **Proverbs 16:9**

Deborah and I believe our plans should be intricately woven in the fabric of God's Kingdom. The adversary would want nothing greater than to derail your journey, so be proactive and intersect his reach. Creating a plan for the sake of our own personal gain would feel void if we did not consider how everything must be infused with our spiritual role, responsibility, and fruit building His Kingdom. When we embrace His ways and judiciously follow written goals or seemingly fall into the right paths, the Father is still directing our steps. Proverbs 16:9 states, "A man's heart devises his way: but the Lord directs his steps." When you write down your plan, include your passion, your purpose and His promises. Then take them before the Father, asking Him to infuse it with His power, His characteristics and traits, so you may integrate all of Him in everything you put your hand to.

Even the Lord made plans, He made a plan for you; Jeremiah 29:11. The book of Proverbs contains many scriptures about planning, counsel, and direction. Thus, when you write out a plan and refer to it often, it is a great plumb line to stay the course as the Lord directs you. The Bible declares in Proverbs 25:2, "It is the glory of God to conceal a thing: but it's the honor of Kings to search out a matter." The honor of a whom? You read it right, a King, he who is entrusted with the government of Heaven upon the earth. That is what God has positioned you for – Kingly opportunities, administrating heavens authority.

HOW DO I GET THERE?

As a person gets an idea and builds on it, God gathers like-minded people to you in areas that complement your skill set. Similar-thinking people will be attracted to the innovation and the heart of that person with an ingenious, God idea. Remember, not everyone gets an idea, but others will have the skills and abilities to help you execute it.

God's creativity in you, will position you to receive the transfer of ideas for this appointed time.

The $64,000 question is, "How do I get there from here?" That is where this book is unique. This is not a self-help book or another call to change-something-about-you. Everything about you has already been conformed to walk with God during this *Shift*. I am confident that the sheer release of *God's creativity in you will position you to receive the transfer of ideas for this appointed time.*

Back in 2000 while I was still a Senior Pastor of a local church, I received a download from the Lord about real estate and mortgages. I bought a few houses in my lifetime, but knew very little about the process. This complex genre includes skills like, how to find the right product; how will you find buyers, and how to prosper especially as a new start-up business. I knew I was not to get a job as a loan officer for a company and work their marketing schemes. That just did not feel right to me as a newbie trying to learn the mortgage business. It was a difficult time in my life and I needed to make some quick adjustments.

Seemingly out of the blue, a man who owned a mortgage business invited me to have coffee. I knew him from when he handled the transaction on my personal residence a while back. We had very little contact since that time, so it was not really an ongoing friendship. Over coffee he shared with me his passion for worship and the desire to pursue that first-love. Over a period of weeks, we came to an agreement where I would own half his business; and he agreed to be my personal mentor in the industry and introduce me to all his contacts and relationships. That is how I transitioned from full-time pastoral leadership and reentered the marketplace, successfully.

The Father paved an avenue for change and then He orchestrated divine appointments. On top of that, Jesus launched me into owning and operating a mortgage office, all without any real capital and no experience. People of like mind and passion joined us and at the end of a two-year period, our business felt more like a spiritual family. We shared vision and shared the workload for the same common goal. Growing a business while ministering to those in the mortgage industry is what God had called us all to do. Although it was not easy, He opened every door. The buyers we worked with were all not only able to find the best mortgage financing, but they found Christ too.

Of course, I experienced many of the challenges a business goes through, including down-turns, deception, and greed. There were, however, a few genuine people working together for the Kingdom cause assigned to us with similar spiritual DNA. Little did I know, this season was in preparation for great exposure and His intentional placement for what is occurring in my life today.

This was birthed from one idea and one divine connection. The influence over lives, and ability to share about Jesus, was astounding, and the sphere of influence grew daily. Sometimes, a business plan is developed and traditional avenues for financing occur. Other times God brings plans and funding through

Keep your eyes open. God's signature of creativity remains thoroughly visible.

sources that would not have been humanly possible to find. Either way, God's signature of creativity remains thoroughly visible. Keep your eyes open. What is God showing you?

SKIN IN THE GAME ... YOURS

A friend of mine, who is also a Christ follower, has been given a wonderful product idea. It is technology that major retailers will want. His company is in final testing to roll-out the product for their first client. It has come at an enormous cost to develop and test, investing two years of his life to bring the project to this point.

My friend is not greedy and is not trying to get rich for himself. He merely desires this product work, benefitting not only the retailer, but their customers. The Lord set him up with the idea, the business partnerships formed were miraculous, and the financing was entirely orchestrated by the Father. This friends' goal is set to use the profits to fund the call of God throbbing in his heart; discipling a generation. The Lord was preparing him to do just that, as this project required him to seek the Lord, interact with similar, Spirit-led people and locate equally yoked, financial backing each step of the way. Whew!

I have often heard believers say the provision of God would come like manna dropping out of heaven. This windfall would not require their time, effort, or personal investment. I am sorry to inform you, this is not like winning the lottery, nor is it a welfare system. His creativity and provision for such is a celestial download where you must invest your time and talents to bring about the desired results. You must have "skin in the game." This is a term we use in the real estate industry. It is when you are in the exact place God wants you to be in, ready to strike, that makes this plan work so well.

You need to be fully invested in your assignment.

We co-labor with God working with passion and personal investment. This is not the same as working by the sweat of your brow without the power of God, but you do need to be fully invested in your assignment. Do you believe you have heard the Holy Spirit? Enough to risk time, energy, and yes, even your bank account? Faith according to Hebrew 11:6 is: "The substance of things hoped for and the evidence of things not seen." This is not quite the same as naked risk, but there is an uncertainty where, in obedience to the voice of God, you are willing to take action before there is any evidence of success.

WHEN SUCCESS FACTORS TURN DOWNWARD

We've observed a consistent pattern networking with Kingdom-minded leaders. As you develop your "God idea," seldom does it progress from conception to profitability in a seamless fashion.

If everything moved forward with ease, I would wonder about the origination of the idea. Nothing comes without work and keeping your hand to the plow. However, God's enemy is called the 'devourer' and he actively consumes Holy Spirit ideas with every opportunity made available by man, to do so. Observe carefully Bible narratives that discuss strategies from heaven, requiring man's involvement. Examples like Josephs dream and then execution of that plan in Egypt, Joshua developing a military strategy and it works. What about Nehemiah and his goal to rebuild the walls of Jerusalem, funded by King Cyrus! There are always challenges and roadblocks along the way, but God delivers.

What happens when everything is in place, you have moved forward executing the plan and one to three years into the process, something turns downward? Was it because of the economy or your business partner? These kinds of stories get repeated all the time. What then? What about the voices inside your head, much less the ones that speak directly in your ear! It can feel like a 'Job' moment. Your heart is prepared, your motives have been tested, and your plans are in movement; then something outside of your control takes over and your "God idea" goes south, or so it appears. Self-doubt comes in, and you begin to question your ability to even hear God, much less convinced He was even in the plan to begin with. Without diving into the millions of specifics that could legitimately play a part here, I want to address *you*.

Remember earlier we talked about stewardship, loosening your grip and personal core values? Now is where all of those come into play. Much like the Word says in Mark 7:14 (summarized), "It's not what goes into a man that defiles him, but what comes out." Herein is that moment!

You see your adversary is not distracted because you bought a business or launched a brilliant idea. Often, I wonder if satan is far more faithful to his goals than believers are. Continual refinement is just that—continual. At every level of this supernatural life, you will be tested, and perhaps revisit, even multiple times, steps of stewardship already discussed in this book. It is a journey and one that requires checks, balances, and maintenance.

Continual refinement means you will be tested at every level of stewardship.

As the enemy proceeds to devour and destroy, we must remain on guard by consistently growing deeper in our relationship with Jesus and paying attention to the details He points out to us. The negative event that you experience may be a test to launch you in deeper places that you have asked God to take you. Or it may be the mercy of God exposing your fears, greed, or pride that needs to be uprooted. It is what comes through a man's lips that reveal what he truly believes. Spoken words bring legal admittance for the enemy to resist or attack your strategies. In exactly the same way, speaking truth aligns you with heavens order, halts satan's actions and releases the outcomes the Father desired.

In preparing for this great *Shift* and throughout the journey, God did not intend for anything to be a one-time event. There is and there will be, a testing of the people of God. We will be tried in the fire of adversity, exposing the core of mankind's deficiencies, greed, jealousy, idolatry, and unforgiveness etc. In order to sustain a place of honor in God's Kingdom, we must come through purified and washed by the blood. We must overcome all the temptations that power and position brings with them and prove ourselves to be true, maintaining a humble and contrite spirit.

As I study believers who influence their culture, there are evidential patterns to their success. You will have no continued effect on people's lives, unless you have weathered the risks. There is no shortcut.

CAN I NOT GIVE IT BACK TO YOU IN A DAY?

On the journey toward this Kingly adventure in the marketplace, we can end up with losses we did not anticipate. Sometimes the vision develops so slowly that it seems non-existent. Loss, the postponement of plans, injured relationships, can leave one disconnected from the dream and even the Dream Giver.

Joseph, just days before promotion, seems to barely hang on to the dream given him early in life. In Genesis, Chapter 40, Joseph interprets a dream and begs the Chief Cupbearer to, "Remember me to Pharaoh, when it is well with you." But the Cupbearer did not remember him. It was two more, long years before the right moment came for Joseph's promotion; and it came to him in *One Day!* During those two years in prison Joseph must have wondered the proverbial "Will I ever see my dream fulfilled?" Have you ever felt this way? This is where true faith and obedience find their value in our continued preparation, we are formed into a vessel that can house the generosity of God.

In 2007, the banking setback virtually ended the direction I was headed with my business. The tragedy of my late wife's battle with cancer and her soon passing, was going on at the same time great financial loss was occurring. I had many questions about the direction my life was headed and whether I should even be in business at all.

One night as I lay awake thinking about my losses, suddenly, this exhilarating impression came to me, "Can I not give it back to you in a day?" Remembering back to that night, He illuminated issues needing to be dealt with in my spirit. What appeared to be loss to me was not loss to Him. The Father reminded me of the fact that He owned everything and what was overwhelming to me is a simple solution for Him. God said that all the things that can consume my time and energy should not have so great an impact on me. The Lord, He is sovereign and His purpose *will* be fulfilled.

I laugh when people perceive me as a great business or financial thinker, as all I have ever really done is just followed the road signs the Father placed in front of me. Oh, I have taken a few detours, and at times I have been in too much of a hurry thus, failing to perform my due diligence. Those I trusted as partners brought results that negatively impacted my efforts; *but God has always gotten me there!*

God will ultimately turn setbacks into advances.

Before the Lord brought Deborah and I together, she had a similar promise spoken to her after a wrenching business loss. The reality remains, we are all on assignment from Heaven and we anchor our hope in His promises and His plan. My friend, *God will ultimately turn setbacks into advances.* The 'Suddenly of God' will come and He will return what was lost with greater abundance. The Lord often brings fruitfulness *while* He is preparing you for greater increase yet to come. Fittingly, the greatest increase of all is developing a true understanding of His wealth as Jesus' character grows inside of you.

HIS RETURN ON YOUR INVESTMENT

Along with the command to 'occupy,' Jesus clarifies His expectation when He said, "I have given all you need to finish the work here." I think He means, "Get *it done!*"

In Matthew, Chapter 25, the giving of talents implies provision. In Luke 19, a different parable than recited in Matthew, where the King distributed talents to his servants, he expected an increase, thus a demand is placed on the recipient. When God supplies tools or resources, He expects a return on the investment (ROI). As we addressed in earlier chapters about stewardship, the Master took the talent away from the steward who did nothing with it. At the very least He expected to earn interest. God was addressing the attitudes of those who are bound in fear. He is not always looking for a large return. He is looking for a mindset and a heart that desires to bring Him increase and growth at whatever level or capacity they are able to do so. With the transfer of His treasure, comes power and with that asset the returns will be astronomical. That is what I believe God has strategized for this moment.

The Father will only require what He has established for you to accomplish. The completed work of the cross gives us legal jurisdiction to take back from our adversary, God's possessions. As you use the talents He gave you, it will maximize your strength and power to occupy. Seize the opportunity. Produce every result you can. For when the Father calls you to accountability, He will be looking for an increase.

WHAT ABOUT THE BENJAMINS?

In our household, we call money 'Benjamins' as in the likeness of Benjamin Franklin on the one-hundred-dollar bill. In our business, we often discern quickly what perspective people have toward "Benjamin" when a possible increase in revenue shows up in a conversation. When I get off the phone with someone, Deborah will jokingly say, "Of course, that was all about the Benjamin's wasn't it?" Indeed. When I read about wealth, I find that most are talking about greenbacks. Real wealth, as stated earlier, is far above the dollar bill. When I experienced a **SHIFT—The Transfer of Wealth**, it was a representation of so much more! The increase of one's bank account is just a byproduct of the change we are now experiencing, certainly not a focus. The significance of what the Father really intends to happen, clearly shows how microscopic money is.

Your view and use of money will indicate your preparedness to hold God's increase and favor.

Needless-to-say, we must discuss money. Although wealth is not reduced to finances, money will play a measurable role in His *Shift*. How you view money and use it, may be a determining factor if you, as God's container, are mature enough to hold His increase and favor. Yes, money is the legal tender in our culture wherewith we live and execute business. Money crosses the path in everything we do, however, it cannot be our priority, nor the end goal. To prove faithful and mature in His Kingdom, entrusted with His transfer, money must never be allowed to seep in and affect our perspective, thus our choices.

1 Timothy 6:10 states, "The love of money is the root of all evil." I propose it's the values and perspectives we hold towards money

that makes it capable for that root to become evil. If your heart is consumed with loving the person of God, the 'now' move will not be driven by a need to acquire more. Instead, it is the transfer of God's authority along with the mature stewardship of His power, that one will use the resources He provides to establish the Kingdom of our Christ within our sphere(s) of influence.

As vessels of God, it is our responsibility to ensure our containers do not become polluted with additives. You know those substances that are added at a later date, that makes the current contents no longer like the original? Those would be called impurities or unapproved additives. The Scriptures are pretty clear on the qualities what we need to avoid. A short list would include greed, selfish ambition, and filthy lucre; 1 Timothy 3:3 (KJV).

GREED by definition is "excessive desire for wealth or possessions."[3] That goes parallel with being a lover of money. It is a pollutant that will stop the flow of God's provision.

SELFISH AMBITION is defined as self-seeking and looking out for one's own interests above anyone else.[4] Another writer states that selfish ambition drives a man to abandon his calling, his family, and his God so that he may satisfy his own lusts. Selfish ambition is often satisfied at the expense of others.

FILTHY LUCRE defined is: Money; originally, money obtained dishonestly.[5]

It is the clever ploy of the enemy to add these pollutants internally in your soul, then again into your business. Not only will those traits damage your witness for the King, it will defile your vessel, give the enemy access to plunder your crop, steal your inheritance and stop short the fulfillment of dreams and desires you once held to fulfill your mandate and bring Jesus His due reward! Those three (3) words can do more damage than you ever want to know.

WHO IS YOUR DADDY?

Does that seem too intimate of a term in addressing Father God? Not for me. Romans, Chapter 8 says that since we have a "Spirit of adoption" our hearts cry out 'Abba Father' or 'Daddy' God. The vulgar use of the term, 'Who's your Daddy,' is not what I prefer, however, it emphasizes what we must *never* forget. God is not only our Provider, He is our exclusive source for everything. He is El Shaddai, the All-Sufficient One.[6] God may or may not use 'man' to provide, but He will always sift your interactions with others through this filter. Our heavenly Father is our Daddy and He has a vested interest in our success on every level.

IT'S ALL ABOUT THE MONEY

It's highly unfortunate that we have reduced the Old Testament, especially the laws of Moses, to children's stories. No, these are glimpses of how our life ought to be. In Deuteronomy 11:13-15, God promises a farming community He will bring rain and will bless their crops. I don't know about you, but if I am a farmer and I get seed, rain and good harvest; I have had a banner year. If this happens year after year, I am a successful business person.

Deuteronomy 28:1-14 lays out the Blessings of Obedience; reasons to desire and need the Father's investment in you and your plans. Take time to fully read His blessing and understand the full measure of why God wants you successful in the marketplace.

So how do you know if God will finance your plan? What the Lord promised and symbolized in the Old Testament has been paid for and made available by Christ as evidenced in the New Testament. As I was faithful to God when He orchestrated the sale and building for Bethel Church on that 71-acre parcel, it was evident that He went above and beyond for us. He brought financing beyond our wildest imagination. He will finance your plans, when you walk in fellowship and obedience to Christ Jesus. Heaven opens and help comes not only to start, but expand your efforts.

Back in 1993 while pastoring Bethel Church in the new facility, the bookkeeping department notified me of a large cash gift that began coming in every week. The amount was very significant for that day and it became a steady revenue stream for our ministry. As a leader and steward of God's resources, I made it a practice not to review the giving records. However, I asked the Father if it was appropriate to personally contact the giver as I felt there was something the Father wanted to teach me. With a sense of permission, I arranged a meeting at a restaurant with the gentleman. I did not talk about money or even say thank you for his generosity. I just asked for his life story.

He was part owner in an airline, based in Southeast Asia and a recent convert to Jesus Christ through our ministry. I was amazed at his lavish heart towards God and obvious brilliance for business. There in the restaurant I prayed for God to give him extravagant ideas and an increase in resources to grow this enterprise. One thing that resonated in me during our brief conversation was that he wanted to be a minister in His sphere of work. Not only was He committed to God being the Owner and the Designer of his business, He wanted to reach out and share the love of Christ with those who worked for him.

Boy was that a refreshing out of the mouth of a recent follower of Christ. After learning about His journey and His goals for the future, I was prompted by the Lord to inquire of reason for His generosity. Emphatically he shared it because of the joy to 'belong'. The environment we cultivated was that of community where everyone participated as a minister of the gospel and not just an observer who came to receive.

God does great work with a heart that is ready for the infusion of His Kingdom. The Father did eventually position this brother to buy other smaller airlines and related businesses. His increase that year was phenomenal. His company grew exponentially as God revealed new strategies to him for more growth. At the same time, God brought increase to our ministry through unexpected and generous contributions much like this one. All of this because we managed the finances of His kingdom well.

God does and will finance His plans for you.

God does and will finance His plans for you, from heavenly resources. He intends to prosper you in ways that are evident to any observer. Wholesome prosperity is refreshing and attractive. Someone who gives God the Glory and remains resolute about the purpose of their business, will draw the attention of the industry they are in. When we walk under an open heaven, not only will there be creative ways to produce revenue, but unexpected and new resources.

Another well-known name in America is that of Hershey's chocolate founder, Milton S. Hershey. Milton modeled the Kingdom in his business. He started the city of Hershey, Pennsylvania as a model for Christian living. His efforts at building a Kingdom business and building the Kingdom of God is one to admire. He was actually an early proponent of an interdenominational work to take focus away from doctrinal differences and apply efforts towards practical Christianity. With a little research, you will discover that God finances His heart in the marketplace.

POSITIONED FOR TRANSFER

How do we position ourselves to encounter this *Shift* in our lives? If you have not heard it yet throughout the book, let me say it again, "It all begins inside of you." Proper positioning always starts internally and progressively moves to the external. Remember the definition of wealth in Chapter 4? We defined virtue, valor and strength. Those are the internal positions. Take note of King Solomon and God's response to him.

In 1 Kings 3:3-14, Solomon is King and is walking in the overflow from his father, David. However, it says Solomon personally loved the Lord and walked in relationship with Him. During a dream, God came to Solomon and asked him, "What can I give you?" What an opportunity here! Solomon reflected on the goodness of God toward his father David, his magnificent inheritance, and then humbly acknowledged his inability to lead Israel as King. He asked for wisdom to judge and rule God's people.

As we have all asked ourselves, "He asked for what?!"

Yes, and because God knew Solomon's heart, which was not self-serving in his request, He would not only would give him wisdom and discernment as asked for, but God went beyond that and gave him honor, riches and a legacy no other King would experience. With a similar heart and attitude, will not the Father grant your desires, your passions, and your requests? Of course, He will.

Seal God's core values on your heart. Prior to Jesus' ascension recorded in Matthew 28 and Mark 16, you discover the proofs of the Kingdom of God within you. Do not expect to succeed in the marketplace without embracing these essentials for your life and your business. The Father will not finance any project without them.

1. **The gospel preached to all nations**. No, you most likely will not preach sermons from your office. The core message of your heart, even when not spoken regularly, is the message of life in Christ evidenced by the currency of Heaven – Love.

2. **The prime directive is people turning to Christ!** Yes, there is a harvest of souls waiting to be won through the life you live and the witness of generosity and kindness that is practiced in and through your life and your actions. It's the kindness of God that leads to repentance; Romans 2:4.

3. **Watch carefully for divine appointments**. My freshman year in college I was coaching at a local school. I always had to go to the school district office to pick up my paycheck. After a year of this routine, I received a phone call late one night and it was the receptionist from the office. There was desperation in her voice and she needed to talk to someone. Every time I went to get my check, I would share a little about my life's goals and would speak some encouragement to her, resembling the love of Christ. Now, in a crisis moment, she turned to a voice of hope and vision. That night, she came to know Jesus.

4. **Miraculous signs following**. It is easy to place all the miraculous evidences of God's Kingdom within the confines of structured church services and mission trips. That is all great, but very limiting to what God has in

mind. I expect miraculous conversion of lives and even systems, in whatever I put my hand to do, when anointed and financed by heavenly resources. His awakening should manifest everywhere you go and in whatever you do. Jesus said, when the blind sees and the lame walk, therein lies the Kingdom of God. It is within you.

5. **Danger prevented!** The last declaration in Mark, Chapter 16 is about serpents and poison. The message sent is God's protection over you, your family, your associates and even your company. As you live the gospel by demonstration, everything you do is protected from any threat that can stop its momentum or its witness.

It's time to step up and into your divine appointment. You have God's heart and will receive His ideas. Start to develop them in prayer and conversation with those you trust. Then watch the Father release and place His blessing on every plan that has His message and His methods in it.

CHAPTER NINE

CONVERGING ANOINTING

How long is a cubit anyway? Most believe a cubit is equal to the length of a man's forearm. That would measure from the tip of the finger back to the elbow. This seems like a rather inexact way to measure distance, at least in our day. Put Tom Cruise's forearm next to Shaquille O'Neal's and you have a large variation for what a cubit length could be. How do you get an exact measurement with such differing variables? How about the value of a shekel as currency? You're grasping what I mean here, I'm sure.

Language is the same way, especially when reading the Bible and the many translations available today. Even words we share in common may carry different meanings due to contemporary usage. Let's look at the word 'King' and what it means to a democratic republic. It does not apply well, does it? When a writer draws a comparison of Christians serving as either a King or a Priest, what does that really mean? It was a much different time and place thousands of years ago. When the teaching about the Kings and Priests rose to the 'hot topic' list for the emerging church, it got me to think. What *was* the Father saying concerning how to be a nation of Kings and Priests, back then and now, today?

KINGS AND PRIESTS A NEW CONSIDERATION

Isaiah says in Chapter 40:31, "But they that wait upon the LORD shall renew their strength; they shall mount up with wings as eagles; they shall run, and not be weary; and they shall walk, and not faint." Do we really believe these words apply to our own spiritual walk even in our culture? Sometimes I wonder! We don't really believe that we are like eagles with keen eyesight and a majestic ability to soar. The Bible is full of allegory. However, I am confident that unlike the eagle metaphor, the Father really does desire for us to apply the words, 'Kings and Priests' literally to our daily lives.

These appellations were intended to help us understand the authority we must walk in. Our God-given titles describe spiritual jobs and authority, bought by the blood of Jesus. If they were meant only as a passing metaphor, the Lord would not have repeated them numerous times in His Word. Kingly and Priestly roles bring order and change to whatever they touch, when we know what God intended them for.

KINGS — As a profession, Kings ruled over the affairs of people and society; a type of government. They made sure the societal structures were in place and functioning well. Kings oversaw the concerns of those who were under their constituency and were responsible to administer and decree justice and order. Kings managed the economy, kept commerce moving forward, set tax rates and policies, and determined the value and type of currency used.

Kings also oversaw a Cabinet or Council of inner circle political advisors and administrators. Furthermore, they directed military operations, war campaigns, and were knowledgeable about the affairs of state and international matters. A Kingly anointing in the marketplace is a spiritual calling to walk with the mantle of authority to *govern over* and increase heaven's resources here on earth. Government and commerce go hand in hand under the Kingly anointing. This mantle has the authority to effect money both within the structure of church or gatherings as we know it, and within the systems of this world.

> **A Kingly anointing is a spiritual calling to govern over and increase heaven's resources here on the earth.**

PRIESTS — Here is another awkward subject for today's Christians. There is simply not a true equivalent in our day to a Biblical priest. The primary responsibility of the Priest was to ensure a correct relationship between God and man. They went before God on behalf of man, and went to man on behalf of God. So, a priestly anointing is the capacity to connect God with people.

1 Peter 2:5, speaks of a Holy Priesthood or, as we would say today, a Kingdom of Priests. They represent spiritual authority revealing God's heart and purpose through us in practical ways, every day. Their duties are functional and necessary for a successful spiritual life. Remember, the priestly anointing is designed to motivate man to stay connected to the Father. Three key parts to that are:

1. **Motivating one another to 'do' good works.** This is action driven like serving. If you want to learn to lead well, learn to serve even better; Mark 9:35.

2. **Praying for one another.** Jesus, as the High priest, makes intercession for us; Romans 8:34. When you pray for people, believing and unbelieving in Jesus, you are functioning as a priest.

3. **Worship ~ Personal and Corporate.** Prayer and worship creates a powerful atmosphere in and over our lives, our cities and regions bringing the Kingdom of God to this earth; one soul, one neighborhood, one business and one city at a time.

The Priestly anointing connects unbelievers to the love of God more intimately and has the authority to link His people to the throne of God where they experience Him. In an article entitled "Two Pillars," Os Hillman confirms the importance of these two critical roles in the activity of the church as western culture understands it.

> *"**He erected the pillars in the front of the temple, one to the South and one to the North. The one to the South he named Jakin and the one to the North Boaz**" (2 Chronicles 3:15-17). What's remarkable is the name of the two pillars that stood in front of the temple: Jakin, which means **it establishes**, and Boaz which means **in it is strength**. Jakin was a priest. Boaz was a businessman also known as a "King" in the scriptures. He was also Ruth's kinsman redeemer whose lineage would be traced all the way to Christ: Matthew 1:5.*

> *It is a picture of two people God used to represent the entrance into God's presence and the forming of the foundation of Christ's Church. The Bible says we are both Kings and Priests, but we also have two separate distinct roles to play in His Body. Kings and Priests are joining together to bring the essence of God into the place that in our evolving culture, has been forbidden territory; the workplace. It is only when this partnership cooperates in unity, mutual respect, and affirmation that we see God's power released. Alone,*

we cannot do it. Together, we can bring the presence of God into all spheres of society to transform workplaces, cities and nations.[1]

Hillman observed that at the very core of Judaism was the connection of the Priest and King. At the most important place of worship, the temple of God, two key pillars were named after a King and a Priest. Pillars speak of strength and foundation. As well, the location of these pillars speaks of the need to work hand in hand, as each supported the rest of the structure.

In the book of Deuteronomy, business was accepted as a spiritual function and given equal importance as spiritual activity for Kingdom advancement. Today, we have displaced the Kings among us within the church. Their activity has been viewed as 'secular' and lower than the priestly function. Recently, a respected member of the clergy referred me to an article that states the function of leaders within the life of the church as greater in God's eyes than the function of the Kingly anointing. Seriously? We have elevated the role of the Priest over that of the King and stifled our greatest potential.

At the most important place of worship, two key pillars were named after a King and a Priest.

I have now served as both Priest and King. The Bible gives clear examples of what can occur when those two functions converge; it creates a chord of strength and sovereignty, difficult to overcome or defend against.

Two remarkable illustrations of this convergence are found in the life of King David and Zerubbabel. David was anointed a King, but also functioned in the priestly role. In 2 Samuel Chapter 6, as King,

David led a worship processional at the return of the Ark of the Covenant to Jerusalem. Zerubbabel, in the book of Haggai, was a Priest who returned with the exiles. Remarkably, he was appointed Governor of Israel and stepped into the Kingly anointing. The Sovereignty of God will orchestrate what is necessary for us today in our culture, so we may administrate His government upon the earth. There is no segregation in the house of God.

HISTORY OF THE CHURCH

The first 300 years of the church literally changed the world. As it says in scripture, "They turned the world upside down." Power and authority flowed in the members of the Kingdom of God as they touched everyone with the redemptive message of Jesus Christ and power of the Holy Spirit. They made such a significant impact upon people and culture that the Roman government had to strategize how to survive the advancement of this Kingdom.

"Not by might nor by power but by My Spirit says the Lord," Zechariah 4:6. This scripture literally applies to the first 300 years of church history. With no army, no resources, and no political backing, and certainly no technology; the early church was changing the world one person, one family, and one business at a time. They massively changed their culture. At this point Emperor Constantine made a political decision to keep this Movement, the new church, from overtaking the Roman Empire.

With no army, no resources, no political backing, and certainly no technology; the early church was changing the world!

History records the assimilation of the church of Jesus Christ into Roman society differently than it appears to me. In one respect, the church being embraced by the Roman culture was a great disservice to the expansion of the message of Christ. In my opinion, Emperor Constantine did not come to Christ as history records. After Constantine saw the "cross in the sky," his behavior showed no relevant change in action or lifestyle. He did not convert to Christianity. Instead, Constantine assimilated the Church into Roman culture and made it a sanctioned state religion; one of several.

What a brilliant political move that was. It is the shrewdness of an emperor who was desperate to remain in power. Soon after this acculturation, the church of Jesus Christ began to lose power, influence, visibility, and the distinctiveness that had advanced their initial movement. The Church simply became like the Romans!

The ability to influence the culture slowly waned as the church disconnected from its mission and methods. With the power of the State to back it up, labeling dissenters as heretics was made easier and the consequences greater. The Hebrew people became dependent on the State for provision and protection instead of their Sovereign God. In later years, in at least one country, the church fought Papal wars and issued Papal "bulls" to prove they had more authority than the ruling monarchs and Kings of the land. The church eventually established its own army and currency. Clearly, and for the most part, the church ceased being organic and became bureaucratized for over a thousand years, until the invention of the printing press. Then the printing of the King James Bible, along with the teachings of a priest named Martin Luther, helped fuel a reformation that continues even to this day.

DISPLACEMENT OF KINGS ELEVATING PRIESTS

By the time we advance to the Reformation, dated by most scholars as beginning on October 31, 1517 in Wittenberg, Germany, the church was nothing like the New Testament community relating to His power and life in Christ Jesus. Spiritual activity and what we deem as 'normal life' did not go hand in hand. The role of Priests was elevated and separated from everyday man. Priests were perceived as one level closer to God than others, and with a higher calling and status. The clergy operated as a class system, developing their own language, titles, legal and educational systems, among other things.

Sermons were delivered and Bibles printed in Latin. Most parishioners could not have read the Bible, even if they had had access to one. Originally, the Priestly role was intended to connect God to man. Rather than fulfilling that role, the Priests actually became a barrier to intimacy and worship and shockingly, even sold indulgences; money donated for permission to 'indulge' in sin, to raise money for their elaborate cathedrals.

Unabated, the Priests of that day preyed on people's ignorance and sense of responsibility for the spiritual welfare of deceased relatives with invented doctrines. The Clergy in Luther's day had stooped to selling "holy relics" which were worthless, imitations and forgeries. So, Luther and a few of his contemporaries began the difficult, dangerous and thankless task of trying to undo a thousand years of pagan culture ensconced within the church culture.

This strange monastic position called a Priest no longer had any resemblance to the real priestly function that was prevalent in the first years of the Kingdom. Yet, God continued to move on, and on occasion Priests still heard the Lord and were mightily used. However, the operations of the church paled in comparison to the early days of its origins when the priestly function applied to every follower of Christ. At the time of Luther, but for a few exceptions, the spiritual life of Christ followers was at an all-time low. Traditional institutions were more religious than spiritual and functioned as an organization rather than an organism. Christ followers in the marketplace were perceived to be secular in their calling, ignorant of the ways of God and needed to bring any increase to the structured church. Those following Christ no longer invaded the world through their everyday life and the separation between 'holy' and 'carnal' (natural) was growing larger.

The execution of business, or any marketplace transaction, was no longer seen as an anointed Kingdom endeavor. Joining the order of Priests was far more important than any other career path and perceived as a route toward upward mobility. Day-to-day life was considered unredeemed, a hopeless existence to be endured until the future Kingdom of God arrived. There was no longer, "Thy Kingdom come, Thy will be done" in earnest.

> **As a royal Priesthood, every believer was to operate in both a King and Priest function.**

What a sad contrast to 1 Peter, Chapter 2 where, as a royal Priesthood, every believer was to operate in both a King and Priest function. Secular life was never viewed as evil. In fact, we were to bring the Kingdom of God into all of life's institutions and win souls daily. Sadly, the church in the Middle Ages had developed a warped version of the Priestly office, not remotely resembling the Biblical design. That model still rules the day. Marketplace believers are still considered subservient to the Priests who labor within the four walls of the organized church.

Kings were permanently displaced as spiritual leaders and, in many circles, that old wineskin, double standard, still exists today. Fortunately, we have had over a half century of a modern, marketplace movement. Demos Shakarian, (Full Gospel Businessmen's Association) became one of the first modernized movements, which, at its height had over one million members. Since then, the number of marketplace ministries in the US has increased from dozens to tens of thousands, and it seems to be a global phenomenon.

One leading Bishop wrote a recent article saying Priests and Kings have different jurisdictions to rule over and each should respect the domain of the other. I don't agree. This carving up of territory and the perpetuation of dualism and schism is sadly wrong, in my opinion. There were no professional clergy or seminaries in the first-century church. All of the original leaders, then called Apostles, were Kings from the marketplace, who became fishers of men and were willing to die for their faith. These were not hirelings. They were true shepherds. That was God's standard then, and it remains the same today.

To summarize, in 1517 a few brave reformists became discontent with what the church had become and risking everything, including their lives, they demanded change. Martin Luther, among others, restored the Bible to the people, printed and distributed, and the revelation of a 'personal' faith. However, the same dysfunctional government of displaced Kings and elevated Priests remained.

REPENTANCE TO THE KINGS

What we are experiencing in the early stages of this *Shift* is that within the common structure of church, we are beginning to understand and operate as the disciples once did. Change cannot come to a world around you, until it begins in you. This is how the birth of the church of Jesus Christ came. Many have tried to bypass that essential first step by allowing Jesus to be Savior, but not Lord of their lives. Internal realignment must precede external effect. Restoring things to the proper order will sustain this *Shift*. Thus, a need for mending the functions in both Kings and Priests; allowing them to work together as indicated in the Word.

Upon my coming to Christ, the call to leadership was confirmed to me by spiritual leaders with whom I had relationship. In the culture where I obtained my training, the Priestly mantle was considered to be the ultimate assignment. My family lineage, interestingly, was embedded in business and entertainment and considered in my new training to be a lower calling. In my early training and even my leadership roles, it was expected that business persons and others not in the Priestly role, would serve on boards and committees, but were plainly perceived as 'second level' or 'second class' spiritual leaders.

Change cannot come to a world around you, until it begins in you.

After several years of laboring, both as a youth leader and Senior Pastor, the Lord lovingly transitioned me into the marketplace. I gained another view very quickly. After surviving the culture shock of leaving pastoral ministry, I soon realized that Kings were dishonored and even disrespected in many traditional religious cultures. For a season, I both pastored and managed mortgage offices and could identify with some of the pains experienced by business leaders, but nothing in comparison to what I learned when I completely left full-time ecclesiastical leadership. The Lord had greater plans for me, and He was preparing me for the journey.

In 2003, I was T-boned from an oncoming vehicle at an intersection on my drive out of town. This accident yielded me many months of pain. My neck and lower back have never been the same even after two surgeries, one of which nearly cost me my life. During the course of all the medical treatment and recovery, I felt it best to step down from full-time pastoring. To model what I believed to be honorable as a spiritual father; I gave away to the leaders in the churches we birthed, mortgage offices I had formed to facilitate revenue for them. To my surprise and due to the perspective that yet remained, it wasn't a gift well-received.

Following a time of transition once I recovered from the accident, I worked in corporate sales positions and did some business consulting work. After a few years of this, it truly felt like a demotion. It was a very different journey and felt much like a dark night of the soul, as the Father began to teach me the necessary changes that I needed to make for what was coming to the Body of Christ.

If I was to break out of the mold and function as both Priest and King, a deeper heart change needed to take place. I did not mouth a 'one sentence' prayer and move on. I searched the Word and it led me toward a different path to ponder and demonstrate. I then went to business leaders that I trusted and began repenting for the ungodly attitudes held by those is the role of Priests.

There is a Kingly anointing and to restore it to a proper role, we must begin with genuine repentance on the matter. For the true transfer to occur, we must restore the Kings among us, beginning with repentance. Living through that season and emerging on the other side as a different person, is what prepared me for the season I am in today.

The Father has taken me to the very arena that He revealed to me back in 2005, which would experience radical change. God told me the mortgage industry was going to collapse. He even positioned me, this time with experience and relationships, placing me directly back into that crisis with great success.

For a true transfer to occur, it must begin with repentance.

The Father has compelled me to share with His Beloved Bride about His heart in this season and for this moment. Every day I live in the blended role of King and Priest. With the experience He has afforded me, my heart cries out for the order of God's Kingdom and repentance due to modern day Kings.

My dear King; as a Priest, I personally would like to stand in, through identifiable repentance to represent all other Priests you have been in contact with, and begin the realignment of heaven for you. I repent before man and God for the subordinate place to which we, collectively, have demoted and demeaned your mantle and calling. You were never intended by the Father to make money to simply serve the needs of His church.

Your calling is so high that the Shift in the current movement of God cannot occur without you. It is you that God has been preparing in secret for years. It is you who have been faithful and diligent, applying God's principles and passionately pursuing His heart into what you were gifted to do.

And, to you who are patiently waiting for the advancement God has promised, He is moving quickly to bring it. What I am speaking of, however, must first come into alignment for that to occur. I am honored to be the Priest/King God has chosen to ask for your forgiveness for our attitudes, actions, and presumptions. I honor your calling. I honor your leadership, your wisdom, and the platform the Father has staged and prepared for you. I welcome you to take your place in the temple of God with honor.

THE NEW TEMPLE, A FINISHED REFORMATION

Reformation occurs when situations need to be rectified back into rightful order. To reform is to change the way things are done. How does it change? By returning to the original plan and operation of the church! The Reformation that began in 1517, caused a significant change, but in my opinion, it was only a partial one. The New Testament model is still lacking in our daily lives today. Key pieces are yet to be fully restored! The restoration of the Kingly mantle and role of Kings must reemerge. The mandate of the kingdoms of this world to become the Kingdoms of our God, necessitates dramatic change. The transformation of societies and institutions of this world must be fully implemented. I believe that all these modifications are now occurring in partial measure, in conjunction to the *Shift* already in motion.

Recent global acceptance and understanding of the priority of the 'Seven Spheres of Influence' and the Kingdom of God, are helping to pave the way and usher in these *Shifts* as we develop common language to dialogue and build around. However, we cannot bring transformation to the positions we occupy and influence, until the reformation from within the four walls of the church occurs.

The restoration of the Kingly mantle and role of Kings must reemerge.

With the reemergence of Kings, a final restoration of the house of God can be anticipated. This is the only institution that will truly bring change to the whole world as God intended. When the Bride of Christ is dressed in the presence of God and fully operational and utilizing gifts and talents released to her by the Father, there is no formidable opposition. Imagine what a fully restored Body of believers must look like? Acts 2:42-47 gives us a memory and model to anticipate what the Church will look like once again.

> "*42 They devoted themselves to the apostles' teaching and to fellowship, to the breaking of bread and to prayer. 43 Everyone was filled with awe at the many wonders and signs performed by the apostles. 44 All the believers were together and had everything in common. 45 They sold property and possessions to give to anyone who had need. 46 Every day they continued to meet together in the temple courts. They broke bread in their homes and ate together with glad and sincere hearts, 47 praising God and enjoying the favor of all the people. And the Lord added to their number daily those who were being saved" (NIV).*

The key ingredients of a fully reformed church appear here in splendor. Christ's followers are:

1. Devoted to the Word; living it and putting it to memory.

2. Sincere about genuine relationships; building community.

3. Involved in rampant and infectious prayer; Unity.

4. Awed at God; living in The Fear of the Lord.

5. Seeing supernatural power every day and everywhere they release His presence.

6. Walking in unity instead of isolation and self- centeredness; humble demeanor.

7. Brimming with gladness and joy permeating their lives and activities.

8. Adorned with favor from the Lord, drawing others to Him.

9. Experiencing legitimate growth; overnight expansion.

10. Bringing change to the city wherein it exists first, then to other regions.

Now that is the kind of Fellowship people would stand in line to participate in. This is a healthy structure, where all believers walk in the power and impact that had previously been observed in just a few, mostly fivefold ministry leaders.

A leadership who did not jockey for position or seek preferential treatment, would govern the activities of this organism. Servanthood and a heart for preferring and esteeming one another would motivate the core leadership. Lack simply did not exist in this unified Body. The Five-fold offices, along with the gifted Bride, would work in agreement and walk together in unison. This reformed Bride would not have to labor to bring transfiguration to the culture she lives in. The sweet aroma of the Bride of Christ exudes from everyone taking his or her place; a ministry on one hand and happily fulfilling their marketplace calling on the other.

A MANY STRANDED CHORD

To bring greater effectiveness to the mission given to all of us—and at the same time, raise the standard against the ploys of the enemy—we must become unified. We do that by creating a fortified front; establishing both an offense and defense.

In military maneuvers, that would be called "taking the flank." In Nehemiah, Chapter 4, when everyone took their rightful position, they were a force to be reckoned with. They worked with a shovel in one hand and were prepared to fight with a sword in the other. Some were situated on the upper level and others on the lower. Nonetheless, everyone participated in the roles they were called to fulfill. They did not bicker over what role they were asked to serve in, they gladly took any position. As a result, the walls went up swiftly. They also had a simple communication system that everyone understood, using the trumpet or ram's horn. It was then and only then that they built a fortress with such efficiency and effect and in only 52 days! That is what a unified front can do. That being said, there are a few other important roles that are required in this upcoming *Shift*.

The office of Prophet is a difficult and yet necessary role in this *Shift*. The assignment God has called Prophets to is not always as exciting or rewarding as some might think. I happen to be married to one and have found I can count on the accuracy of 'a word' time and time again. This accuracy of course, comes with years of seasoning and personal maturity. If I veer off the course even in the slightest direction, God is faithful to bring clarity and course correction quickly. I so appreciate that as we walk daily, seeking God's direction and staying in unity, the day unfolds like a flower and we walk in a peaceful and strong cadence.

Prophets were indispensable in Bible times. Their roles have changed with cultural *Shifts*, but not their gift. The Office of Prophet is one in and of itself is pivotal for strategy, it brings spiritual alignment, and provides foreknowledge of what is to come. Today, many function in the prophetic anointing and are being used by the Father to help guide, pray, and war against the plans of darkness. They too can function in strategic methods and foreknowledge of what the Father would say. They must not be ignored but through relationship employed by leaders to help in the *Shift* upon us.

Although the term **intercessor** is not listed as an office, or five-fold function in scripture, they most definitely exist. In 1 Timothy 2:1-2, Paul writes of the diversity in praying, specifically the role of intercession. Throughout the Bible, the prayers of saints have gone before the Father and dramatically made a difference. As Paul Billheimer so appropriately states in his book, *Destined for The Throne*[2], everything God does on the earth is *directly in response to prayer*; from the Sun standing still, to the rain ending a drought, to a release of angelic warfare on behalf of Daniel.

> **The Prophetic is pivotal for strategy, it brings spiritual alignment, and provides foreknowledge of what is to come.**

The authority that Christ followers carry in heaven and on earth has not yet been fully tapped by the believer, awaiting his engagements in the heavenlies. More and more we realize that the continual and effective pursuit of the Father's heart toward man and culture, must take place on the path established through prayer. Today, many Kingdom entrepreneurs in the corporate world are building whole prayer strategies around the success of their business. Taking territory in the heavenlies to establish on the earth is a team effort and when unified, brilliantly works.

As prayer paves the way, the Prophets and prophetic gifts keep us on the right path. If we look at previous moves of God and significant spiritual *Shifts*, we find they often fade over time. Reading about them today, it is easy to see where failure occurred. The most predominant reason is that the Body of Christ gets easily sidetracked. The tendency to divert from the path God established has been the downfall of previous movements. Since A.D. 300, no two generations have sustained a move of God equally, much less experienced a multigenerational revival or taking dominion as so ordered of the Lord and demonstrated by the early church. Remaining true to the work of the Holy Spirit, while taking more ground for the Kingdom, is vital. This requires integrating the work of the prophetic.

When someone gets distracted or pulled in a direction not authorized by the Father, a prophetic ear can hear from the Lord how to bring clarity or confirmation. Business strategies now include employing prophetic intercessors who stay close to the center of development, assisting leadership to remain true to the 'God idea' and mission.

The Intercessor paves a straight path and the prophetic keeps us on the course developed and directed by God. David was spared much disappointment by seeking the wisdom of Nathan the Prophet, who brought the word of the Lord to his King. The most memorable of these prophetic words was when David was instructed not to build the temple. This *Shift* will only be sustained if we add the mantles and anointing of the Intercessor and the Prophet to those of the King and Priest. This unification establishes a Holy border, and empowers us in the name of Jesus Christ to tear down strongholds and take back High places occupied by our enemy. Jesus took back the dominion, given to the adversary by man's choices. He expects us to engage the *Shift* with full authority and establish His dominion in our cities. We can advance the Kingdom as a unified Bride if we will make the change God desires to orchestrate in our day.

THE FORMIDABLE FORCE OF UNITY

We have taken a brief look at some essential components in the current move of the Holy Spirit. The *Shift* involves the restoration of all the necessary parts to fulfill the original plan. Convergence is often used to describe a necessary coming together of essential parts. It is the creation of a 'sweet spot' that causes the catalyst of change.

The reemergence of the Kingly mantle, honored equally at the level of a Priestly anointing, is the catalyst in the Kingdom for our generation. A full *Shift* will occur as intercession and the prophetic take their rightful role in the *marketplace*. Looking at God's original plan for full refurbishment, it all seems so clear. With a passion to restore all things created by the Father, a convergence occurs and alignment is established.

Unity becomes a formidable force against darkness when the restoration of Biblical assignments is fully functioning.

Unity becomes a formidable force against darkness when the restoration of Biblical assignments is fully functioning. All the pieces coming together in one place and working side by side, is already happening. The necessary connection between the Bride of Christ and their functional role within our culture has begun. This spiritual *Shift* within the church requires action.

As the right change agents, we have been prepared and entrusted. NOW receive the transfer of wealth and influence that has been waiting in the storehouses and treasuries of Heaven. *Step into your role, with full dominion and authority and advance His Kingdom; Matthew 11:12, "From the days of John the Baptist until now, the Kingdom of Heaven has been subject to violence, and the violent lay claim to it."*

CHAPTER TEN

THE PERFECT STORM

In October 1991, when Hurricane Grace combined with mid-latitudinal air masses in the North Atlantic, what emerged was a scenario that became famous both in Hollywood and in literary form known as "The Perfect Storm."[1] All the conditions lined up and moved with such momentum, that the inevitable happened. Not even the seasoned of sailors could control the savage waters they found themselves caught in. Even in an effort to retreat, they turned directly into a rogue wave. These exceptionally skilled men could not navigate through the conditions they found themselves in.

Much like the crew of the Andrea Gayle in the movie, this generation has been caught unaware. All of this is perfect timing for the Bride of Christ to take her place. Unlike their situation, which lead to swift and sudden disaster, with Christ at the helm; He will navigate His Bride through these tumultuous waters. Not only will He provide a solution, but direction for the world at large.

A RUNWAY FOR THE BRIDE, NOT A RUNAWAY BRIDE

For centuries, the Bride of Christ has been, in some cases, a 'no-show' on the stage of world transformation. Rather than taking the lead in the human theater, she has opted to stand on the sideline. With excuses, petty theologies, and a sundry of other reasons, many have become like the guests who were invited to the wedding feast in Matthew, Chapter 22. They are the ones who are sidelined from the real action because of other commitments. Too often it would appear, the Bride votes in abstention, fleeing from her assignment much like Jonah did.

Rather than taking offense to that comment, there should be a willingness to be honest and look at the overall state of what the 'church' could be. Let us open our hearts and ears and begin to seek the Father about our place and our role in all of this. Let us decide we are going to accomplish what has been asked for us to be and do. We will not be sidelined anymore, for any reason.

We are the representation of the Kingdom of God here on the earth.

God's desire for us has been presented again through another invitation for the Bride to take her place and not only attend the wedding feast, but lead others to it. The Body of Christ must decide that her call is more than merely attending Sunday services and sharing fluffy prophetic words. We are *the* representation of the Kingdom of God here on the earth. We have been given, in the marriage contract, i.e., salvation, all the rights, privileges, and authority to administrate God's Kingdom here on the earth, right now, during our lifetimes.

All dressed up with places to go, we must choose this path with a purposeful perspective. Keeping your eyes fixed on the prize, is a view and commandment that focuses your attention and encompasses all that is right in front of you. We can no longer be farsighted or nearsighted, but must see clearly with spiritual eyesight. We must be soldiers, looking every day for great doors of opportunity, marching forward to complete God's assignments. Wherever those assignments may be, at home or during business; simply ask the Lord daily what His will is in every situation you find yourself in, and then do it.

WHEN CONVERGENCE HAPPENS

It is deeply appreciated how much wisdom comes forth regarding Jesus' anointing. I am reminded in Isaiah 10:27, "The yoke shall be broken because of the anointing." There is a yoke of bondage over this world, on the economy and those participating in it. We marketplace Christians had very well believe we are carrying the anointing, under the canopy of God in this great pursuit. Through our obedience to the Father's heart, we are breaking individual and corporate bondages. We can develop strategies to successfully transition the power and influence over commercial arenas, where our adversary has been in charge far too long.

Remember, convergence speaks of things coming together. God's will, coinciding with our will, create the environment where His anointing is "smeared on" and "rubbed over" all our actions and ideas. In fact, do not move forward in any activity without God's anointing. The Lord states in James 4:13-14 summarized, that it is unwise to plan business endeavors on your own strength and neither approved or anointed by the Holy Spirit. No, every plan and strategy should have heaven's seal of approval upon it. The convergence we seek before everything else, is the coupling of our heart with the Father's heart. The anointing is the "sweet spot."

MAKING MONEY IS HOLY

One of the misnomers in Christian thought today, is defining what is Holy and what is common or even profane. In Romans 14:14 it states, "I am convinced, being fully persuaded in the Lord Jesus, that nothing is unclean in itself. But, if anyone regards something as unclean, then for that person it is unclean." Although this particular passage is addressing what people eat, a greater application encompasses all things created by God. Many have considered earning large amounts of money unholy and unsanctified.

Many of my contemporaries have taken this thought to the **Success is holy and Increase is holy!** farthest extent by saying anything done outside of the auspices of the local church, is less holy than what happens within the four walls of the church. I want to set you free and disabuse you of thought and belief! *Success is holy and Increase is holy!*

The words holy and sanctified come from the same Greek root word. *Hagiazo*[2] is a verb denoting the act of purifying or consecrating. *Hagion*[3] is a noun used to describe something has become holy or sanctified.

The usages explain that there is a process to something common or profane becoming holy or sanctified. When money comes your direction that is from an unholy source or use, it can become sanctified and holy because:

1. You are the righteousness of God, in Christ Jesus. Therefore, by the redemptive blood of Christ it can be purified and change jurisdictions. Thus, a holy transfer.

2. A seed can only reproduce of its own kind. Therefore, make sure your actions and your relationships are of holy intent and purpose.

The anointing on your life and your actions sanctifies the results of increase. Then by the virtue of where it now is used, it becomes

"Hagion," or holy money because it is now a part of the Kingdom. Money in a person's life takes on the morality of the user. As a follower of Christ in this culture, we are to bring true holiness to whatever we touch. When we introduce someone to Christ they become the "holiness of God" or set apart for the Father's purposes. As we grow wealth, the resources acquired become holy because God is taking from the unrighteous to bring increase to the righteous.

When Israel won a battle, they set the spoils aside for the Lord's purposes, unless God had specifically commanded them to be destroyed. When we engage in enterprise, acquire assets, or have money come into our possession, it is all holy by His design and even more by our use of it. It is the intended use of money that determines spiritual value.

It's the use of money that determines Spiritual value.

I have seen Godly people use money in an unholy manner and nonbelievers use money in a holy fashion. That is why you often see an unbeliever reap Biblical benefits. The unbeliever can use money in alignment with Biblical principles and reap the spiritual reward. Or, a believer who uses wealth for personal or selfish gain, can open access to the devourer in their life. The best thing that can ever happen with wealth, is to have it come into the hands of a righteous person, who has their heart purified and purposed to glorify God and expand the Kingdom.

Part of heaven's orchestrated change for this season has to do with the transfer of unholy endeavors to holy enterprise. I bought a property once from someone whose goals were diametrically opposed to everything I lived and believed. I knew very quickly that some of his goals for money were in conflict with the Kingdom. When I purchased the home at literally 25 cents on the dollar, the profits were extracted from hands that would have used it for goals contrary to the heart of God. Now, the profit was in the Kingdom and could be used for Kingdom advancement. The profit I earned was set-aside for the Lord and it became holy. The key factor is, I set it aside and inquired of the Lord. I did not celebrate 'my' gain but His as I determined in my heart, all of what I have is given to me to use as He so directs me to do so.

There are major spiritual and financial advancements when profit, intended for an unholy cause; sex trade, drug cartels, terrorism, Mafia, is entrusted into the hands of the righteous. That money becomes empowered releasing a *Shift* in the heavenlies and over a society where it is now used to bring redemptive power and purpose.

FACING OUTWARD

One of the greatest schemes our adversary achieved was to convince the Body of Christ to isolate themselves from the 'world' and turn inward as they separated themselves. This was almost as clever a maneuver as suggesting to Adam and Eve to eat of the Tree of the Knowledge of Good and Evil so they would be like God. A basic strategy of warfare is deception, or drawing your enemy's attention away from their intended focus. One of my all-time favorite books I was required to read during my philosophy class in college was entitled, *Christ and Culture.*[4] At the time I had little interest in it and found it difficult to read. In retrospect, I realize it was one of the most important books I would have been exposed to. The message was to help us identify in various ways how Christians view culture and their participation in it.

For too long, the church has stood in a circle holding hands and facing inward while missing epic opportunities set before them. The one exception has been the release of professional spiritual leaders and America's great missionary enterprise. That has been the shining star of our religious history. Few deliberate advancements have been made otherwise. Most of what we celebrate, is the size or number of our churches. This is pure myopic sadness!

We are the righteousness of God in Christ Jesus to people and societies in need of redemption. Building business is rooted in that same righteousness. Equipping Kings for release into the community is a marvelous place to start. It gets our focus off the local house and back on to the world. The same holds true for schools, hospitals, ad infinitum. A culture does not become transformed simply by our presence, but through the presence of God in us creating an atmosphere for change. Jesus said in John 12:32, "If I be lifted up I will draw all men unto me."

A culture becomes transformed through the presence of God in us creating an atmosphere for change.

As a teenager I worked at Irwindale Raceway, then owned by the founder of In-N-Out Burgers. I had the privilege to meet him a couple times and knew he was deliberate about his witness. Committed? Just look under their cups. Every cup is stamped with a scripture on it. That franchise is successful everywhere and the imprinted scripture has not hindered sales. Instead it seems to have brought favor on their endeavors. These are 'tribes' who have decided to face outward. They have declared with their actions, 'We are children of God and those who have contact with us will know, in a diversity of ways, about Jesus and His love for them."

It is in our DNA to do so. Christ's followers should be the most creative of all groups of people and we should be *the* standard of integral employees that serve their employers with excellence. Businesses should be lining up to hire the people of God and receive the blessing and favor that lie upon them and are associated with their righteousness.

A FIVEFOLD SHIFT

Another great development in recent church history is the changes in the five-fold ministry; leadership building the foundation for others to succeed on. The 'Pastor' and the 'Evangelist' have been accepted and embraced for decades. The decade of the 80's was the time where the 'Teacher' took on prominence. The 90's of course was the return of the 'Prophet' in full force. The new millennium began with the open development and acceptance of the 'Apostolic' among us. The Bible states in Ephesians 2:20 –22 *"…built on the foundation of the apostles and prophets, with Christ Jesus himself as the chief cornerstone. [21] In him the whole building is joined together and rises to become a holy temple in the Lord. [22] And in him you too are being built together to become a dwelling in which God lives by his Spirit."*

With the five-fold coming into proper order, the house God has designed will withstand and overcome any storm. A requirement for our generation is that our spiritual house must have the foundational work and leadership of the Apostles and the Prophets in the right place. What is yet to be more clearly understood is how they all fit together.

Most of the time, the Apostles and Prophets are on the roof of the house, not laying its foundation as indicated in scripture. That is partly due to their recent acceptance within the current structure of traditional church. It is also due to corporate structure being in place more often than genuine Kingdom relationships. The

Father is bringing all that into alignment. God's house must have a fully functioning leadership to equip the saints for this immense opportunity. As both leadership and equipping matures rapidly, the Kings in the house can go forward with freedom and support. As the house comes into order, the "saints go marching on," taking territory as He so planned.

WHEN KINGS GO WITH BLESSING

With the government of God in place, the next vital step must be taken and taken quickly. In step with the Holy Spirit, Kings must be commissioned with a blessing to fulfill their destinies. Previously we embraced corporate repentance for having Kings take a lesser role than originally chosen for them by God.

Our next step would be to have a strategy for the equipping and releasing of these marketplace leaders now that we see Kings as a holy role and what they do is indeed ministry. Taking it one step further, let us follow the pattern of scripture and anoint them with prayer and send them out with our blessing. Let us send the Kings out as Holy Spirit Ambassadors, expecting the miraculous to follow their words and actions.

Send the Kings out as Holy Spirit Ambassadors, expecting the miraculous to follow their words and actions.

If you are a Priest, I suggest you gather the Kings in your house and together collaborate for a strategy for Kingdom expansion in the marketplace. If you are a King, as a leader, I suggest you pull the Kings together and if supported by a Priest, ask them to assist you. If not, you can lead this as a 'Priest' for your tribe. Surround them with intercessors and bring the relationship to a higher level with true prophetic voices. Create partnerships between the 'for profit' and the "not-for-profit' entities. Instruct the Kings as to the nature of their calling and structure strategy. After training; lay hands on them, anoint and commission them to prepare to walk under an open heaven. Crucial to the transfer forthcoming, connect them to the Father *and* the heart of spiritual leadership; then send them out with the Father's covering and blessing.

JOINT VENTURE WITH GOD

As the Priests empower Kings in the house of God to move forward into their called sphere, we must sanction them to joint-venture with God. A joint venture is where two parties make an agreement to accomplish a specific business strategy. Each party in this venture comes with unique abilities or assets necessary to achieve success. Often, one party brings the capital, while the other party brings the plan, and the sweat to make it happen.

A joint venture is a mutually agreed upon concept that is written, signed, and executed by both parties.[5] One truism that always seems evident with any and every joint venture is, "No savvy investor brings money to the table unless they like the strategy and are convinced it will succeed." Likewise, our Father invests only in success stories. That means with God as a partner, coupled with His expertise, He has provided for us the necessary means for success. Because God is all knowing, He never fails. The only way we can fail is not to follow His directives, as seen in the parable of the talents.

There is no guesswork with God. Many of Christ's followers have good ideas for creative business success, but never seem to get the capital needed to launch or advance their project. This is the proverbial "so close and yet so far away," and applies to many Christians with an idea. Why would God finance some ventures and no other creative strategies? The answer is far simpler than we realize! If God is the financier of a project, He must be in agreement with all the pieces of your strategy, including the timing to roll out.

For God to agree to, and sign off on a project, it must be in compliance with Kingdom goals and principles. Do you think that all the Father cares about is making money or making your life better? Yes, you can have a profit-making plan and even become wealthy through it, but any project God will infuse capital into must have, in its DNA and execution, a mandate to change lives and alter the culture. That is the third dimension to a Kingdom enterprise that is often overlooked.

> **For God to sign off on a project, it must be in compliance with Kingdom goals.**

Some believers consider compliance with Kingdom goals is to simply put a fish symbol on all your materials and brand it. Nothing could be further from the truth. Neither do you have to say, 'God bless you' every time you have a sale. What is indicative of Kingdom influence is generosity, love, care and concern of others, supporting the widow, the poor, and creating an inheritance for the next generation. These are reasons you desire to engage in business. That does not mean the scope of your business is the poor or the widow, but what is embedded in your productivity is that wealth from your operation invests in those areas that are near to God's heart. This is a joint venture and both parties must agree to the use of profits. When you become His hand extended, He will release even more!

In this *Shift*, the storehouses of heaven are opening in unprecedented creativity that has Kingdom DNA all over it. God has provided for it all! The strategy and the finances are built into these plans, but the Lord wants us to sign on to necessary components, ensuring the success of what He loves. Essential elements for the *Shift* to occur is that the growth of the Kingdom is the goal and enterprise is His chosen vehicle to bring it.

Business is an exciting place to be as a Christ follower, if you have God as a joint-venture partner. Exciting is an understatement, if you are ready to partner with the Father to bring His heart into the equation. Many enterprising Kings have signed onto the goal of eternal life! A few more have signed onto the idea of life and business as a ministry, but most have missed the third and essential piece of the joint venture; where business *is* ministry. It's the place that can demonstrate with action the heart of a generous and sacrificial God.

Every Kingdom-endorsed plan involves the principle of God's heart as described above to bring heaven's culture to the earth. This includes your devotion to His core values. I apologize to those this will shock, but the first changed life should be yours! This requires us to sign onto heaven's plan to invade all the spheres of influence with the message of Jesus Christ. We are not of the world, but we are in it and we are in it to share Jesus with others. Separation and isolation is not God's plan. It is man-made to the core. The financial increase belongs to Him and if you hold the gain in an open hand allowing Him to direct where you place it, you will experience what King David did; an unending supply.

A CADENCE MARCH

Galatians 5:25 says, "If you live in the Spirit, then keep in step with the Spirit." God's simple comment here tells us that we can be Spirit-filled and yet not aligned or in tune with *the* Spirit. The Greek word, "*stoicheo*" for "in step," actually depicts soldiers walking in sync with the troop leader.[6] It is a cadence step that is inflected here.

When He moves, we move. Our lives are to be in a cadence march with the Lord Jesus Christ as our King and commander. Creative, successful believers should not be the exception. They should be the norm. The Lord is on a mission to change those statistics. Jesus has opened the heavens above us. God *Shifted*, aligned and converged the very economic and cultural situations to plant you, with blessing and favor, here right now. We must have and possess a listening ear and an obedient heart.

You can and will prosper by staying in step with the Holy Spirit. *The next great move of God will not be contained within the structure of traditional church, but in the streets of the city, the highways of business and the roads where life intersects.* It is coming to the world through you and unbelievers will no longer have to search for a church house to find Jesus. The House is coming to them as you are the temple of the Holy Spirit; join His army. Walk where the Spirit steps and nowhere else. The trumpets of heaven have sounded the march and we must get in sync with the Spirit to both receive and sustain God's favor and blessing. This is the time to show forth the glory of the Lord.

UNLEASHING HIS PROVISION

Remember, we are of another Kingdom and a separate economy managed by Heaven. We are in the world, but not of the world. Companies like Hershey's sell chocolate and prosper regardless of the state of the economy. See this as a glimpse of what should be a regular occurrence among Kingdom strategists. As World War II was closing, supplies dropped over the nations of the Pacific always had a bar of Hershey's chocolate. The company prospered. Hershey's became a Godly witness by how they treated employees i.e., the generosity of the Father.

The favor the company enjoyed, served as a powerful witness as the Asian world, along with the troops of the United States armed forces, ate chocolate from a Kingdom-minded business. Favor and anointing spread to the world through the Hershey company. Then as Hershey's prospered, they developed a diversity of products and created more businesses.

All this occurred because a Kingdom man named Milton Snavely Hershey kept the mandate of the Father ever before him. As his company stayed true to God's mission, heaven unleashed provision. The only reason why some of the goals of the company ended were due to a change in the business model and leadership after Hershey's death. The same advancement, anointing, and financial effect is true with other ministry-minded businesses such as Hobby Lobby and Chick-Fil-A to name a few. Creative and innovative ideas for business and even for life in general, are the direct result of devotion to the heart of God for our nation and the world.

> **The storehouse of heaven will open up a deluge into the storehouse of those containers built to hold the glory of God.**

When your plan possesses God's heart and methods, you unleash His Provision. The storehouse of heaven will open up a deluge into the storehouse of those containers built to hold the glory of God the Father in Jesus Christ. The same was true of R.G. LeTourneau, the famed "mover of men and mountains," whose heavy equipment was used to build the Alaskan Highway and to clear jungle landing strips in the South Pacific during World War II. Although an eighth-grade dropout,

LeTourneau's name is listed on over 300 patents in the U.S. Patent & Trademark Office. His philosophy was, "There are no jobs too big, only machines too small." LeTourneau is equally famous for giving 90% of his income to the work of ministry and living on the remaining 10%, as was famed James Cash Penney, aka J.C. Penny.

The current transfer of wealth and influence will bypass many because of wrong desires and theological ideologies. You must possess God's perspective and heart to receive this release of glory and favor. You might say, 'But I need to discover how to find the capital to begin my adventure.' That is a common concern. My response would be, "What are you doing in your adventure that is or will grow the Kingdom? What core values has God forged in you to make room for in exchange for **Shift—The transfer of wealth** and influence that you are seeking? What is the testimony you can share bringing Jesus His due reward?" I am confident, that before one will be entrusted with this place of authority or transfer, they must be able to answer those fundamental questions. Then, the storehouse of heaven, will *Shift* to your house.

Deborah has a dear friend in California who managed millions of dollars for large companies that if mentioned by name, would be familiar to you. In the course of success and power, that gentleman gave room to pride. Confident in and of his own abilities, he pushed the edge a bit too much and ended up taking a fall in a financial measure for 'the team.' After a few years in prison and undergoing a complete character change, he began feeding the hungry people in his city. He set up food distribution throughout Southern California. Simultaneously, he opened discipleship and training homes for those transitioning out of prison or living in unfortunate situations. His core training is simply Jesus. He works directly with them, involved in their personal lives and choices. Opportunity comes to them as their character becomes more like the heart of

Jesus. With his sleeves rolled up, he is building men and women and helping to transfer lives from the kingdom of darkness to the Kingdom of Jesus Christ.

During the last few years with the economic challenges, this brother's food distribution business was in need of a serious infusion of capital. Giving was down and donations had waned. However, the need for assistance was on the rise. More people were hungry, and even more in need of personal discipleship. Does this sound like your community? Daily, our friend would come before the Lord and seek direction, but much of his time was spent giving and doing for others. He was not running around looking for donations. Even when facing the loss of his own home to foreclosure, he stayed true to his heart. "It is all the Father's anyway. He will give and He will take away. I am here to do what he has set before me to do." He said.

Then, through Deborah, the Lord gave him a prophetic directional 'word'. It was the first time they met and she knew nothing about his business much less his needs. It was not a 'new' word to him, because the Father had spoken it directly to him twice that morning in his devotional time. This was now a third confirming word. However, inclusive of that message was the Father's blessing that he had been tried and proven to show the character of Christ. You see, this man had laid down his financial gift. His ability to make money was truly a gift from heaven. However, he so wanted to never return to the man he once was that he refused to engage in the very arena he was created to rule over.

When we hear God's delight over us, it resonates deeply in our spirit. The awareness of His affection and approval brings a release to walk through the veils of fear we have held onto and seek His directive to move forward.

We are not to hold back the talents we have. We are simply to step into it with God's direction. From that day forward, the doors began to swing wide open for Deborah's friend. Previous financial relationships called from out of nowhere. He served others, setting up a business assisting people with mortgage loan modifications so they would not lose their homes. He never negotiated a contract for personal remuneration, he merely used his gifts to bless another and assist those at risk. When asked about his concern for compensation, he told Deborah, "Don't worry, the Lord will reward me."

Since then, the wealth of the world he once played in was made available again. He may have taken a break in the business realm he was called to, but his associates kept increasing in business. When God restored relationships, it was as if he never missed a beat. His Godly character is a witness and influences the many investors that come to him for private management. His food distribution service is stronger than ever and supported by businesses and the community around it. His discipleship homes have all increased. The local government has given him homes to use for an exchange of $1 per year to increase his ministry outreaches. The city police force has trained him and his spiritual sons in security measures and enforcement. The expansion of God's Kingdom was evident in all he did. This is a man who has been tested, tried, and reinstated with a heart that lives only for Jesus.

One of the largest countries in the world that possesses no inclination towards God, has sought his assistance to become financially stronger and request his help in developing a service to feed their poor and needy. Talk about favor, influence, and provision! He went from the prison to the palace, just like Joseph did in Egypt. When you follow God's plan and nurture a heart to walk in His mission, heaven's storehouse is unlocked on your behalf and miraculous provision flows to glorify His Son. This is just one, among many contemporary examples of the *Shift*; transferring the wealth of heaven to you for His plan!

HIS OVERFLOW OF ABUNDANCE

"My God shall supply all of my needs according to the riches of His glory in Christ Jesus," Phil. 4:19. "I have given you life and life more abundantly," John 10:10. The word *abundant* is the Greek word "perissos" meaning excessive, exceedingly, beyond, and advantage.[7] Nothing the Father does is in lack or is even in moderation. We see extravagance and abundance in all the Father participates in. From the first day of creation to the new heaven and earth, we read of overflow. People who have visited heaven or have dreams and visions of God's throne room, speak of creative colors, life, all circumstances expressing *abundance.* Others who talk of the 'Treasury Room" of heaven stipulate unending mounds of gold, gold coins and stacks and stacks of bricks. It's not like He lacks anything as He made it all.

   Both scriptures are intentionally placed at this point in the book. The operative words here are **glory** and **abundant**. I am committed to authentic exegesis. This means the context of any statement must be consistent with the meaning of the passage. Any extrapolation must be congruent to truth where this subject is spoken of beforehand in the Bible.

   Ask yourself why have there been times of abundance in some Kingdom endeavors and then other times not? In my opinion, it has to do with whether a heart can be entrusted or not with Who God is. Which leads me to the second word: **Glory.** The Greek word Paul used here is "doxa" which translated means dignity, honor, praise, and worship.[8] The Father does not release abundance to just anyone or anywhere. No, there is concern with who will receive the glory. Scripture teaches that abundant supply is according to His glory in Christ Jesus. Jesus brought full glory to the Father's name. In remaining consistent with that model, will *we* bring glory to the Father?

I wish I had time to tell you of the many people we have met and love already living in this *Shift*. They are currently walking in the transfer of wealth of influence and resources in thrilling measures. These stories and examples are increasing rapidly. Of those I know personally, they are committed stewards of both their possessions and of that dressed in His glory. They want His kingdom expanded and they want men and women everywhere to serve and worship the Lord Jesus Christ. They claim ownership over nothing and refuse to share in the credit reserved only for the Father. They hold on to all they are doing loosely and would give it away and start again if the Holy Spirit so moved them to do so. These are true Kings and Priests as modeled in the Old Testament and confirmed with the New Testament.

With each step of obedience, God opens new doors of opportunity. Delightfully, God literally gives more talents and subsequently more places wherewith His Kings will use them. Our life is to be a holy conduit of supply and abundance overflowing with His joy. While our world *Shifts* downward, we are *Shifting* upward demonstrating the extravagance of the Father – not unto ourselves – but to the Glory of Christ Jesus, the Son.

CHAPTER ELEVEN

AFTER YOUR TRANSFER

IN IT FOR THE LONG HAUL

The *Shift* is not an end of a long-awaited season, nor a one-time event. It is the beginning of what has been anticipated for a very long time—a positioning of the Bride to fulfill her destiny. Many times, before, we watched God align His people to build and advance what was started long ago. The *Shift* has begun and it behooves us to establish all that He has ordered. We are anointed to *establish* and *advance* what has been entrusted to us. This requires the wisdom not only to sustain it, but to generate growth that will last from one generation to the next.

Few organizations have been or become multigenerational. Although operating strong, they rarely resemble the original model. The Father has orchestrated the *Shift* at this moment in history, to position His Kingdom; not only for the transfer of power and authority, but to our generation's epitaph. Proverbs 13:22 address this specifically, "A good man leaves an inheritance to His children's, children; but the sinners wealth is stored up for the righteous."

What will be written in the libraries of heaven about this age in history? To be born for such a time as this, is an honor. To be a part of the greatest establishment on earth, is humbling. However, to do so with grace and direction will build the infrastructure intended to support all that God has begun and increase every facet of life and with a measurable gain. This will begin a sign pointing to a great harvest of souls; one the Father has waited much too long for.

In 2 Peter 1: 3-10, Peter identifies character traits and Godly attributes that prevent us from becoming blinded to long-term goals. Specifically: goodness, knowledge, self-control, mutual affection and love. And of course, Jesus demonstrates by His actions that the greatest of these is Love. Our focus should remain on developing an increasing measure of these traits. The Father expects that to happen in sync with Him. It is a shoo-in.

The transfer is in motion. The reserve of all that we need has piled up for His Bride to lay hold of as a part of her mantle. Momentum has grown. *Shift* is going to happen. He is only interested in those who are ready to participate and at what level. His ready Bride is going to rise to this significant new season. She will embrace with great joy what the Father has planned and determine that the generational inheritance will be consistent with the Originator's intent.

SURPRISE! MORE THAN YOU COULD IMAGINE

Drop a pebble into a pond and it creates a ripple effect that continues until it fades onto the shore. When there is a *Shift* on the ocean floor, the movement of the earth's crust supporting the body of water, creates a reaction. Under the right conditions, that reaction can result in a tidal wave or even a tsunami.

This kind of a *Shift* can move hundreds of miles, quickly reaching distant shores without warning. Our current *Shift* is intended to cause a similar effect. This transition is not limited to momentary increases, but more importantly, designed to stamp a lasting imprint that the Father, once again, will demonstrate Himself in such magnitude, that His name will be recognized in all the earth as he releases an unstoppable motion for those who will partner with Him and change the landscape in this hour. Whether this *Shift* begins as a ripple in a pond, or emerges as a tidal wave from the crust of the earth, will depend entirely on your cooperation with Him.

By this point, you have become familiar with my fondness for physical law demonstrating spiritual truths. Using another example, I'd like to take a look at how water percolates in downward motion. The theory I am referencing is that water will always seek the lowest level. A close friend of mine had a lovely house overlooking the Sacramento River. When visiting, I always enjoyed looking out over the river and taking in the view. Once while gazing out at a rainstorm, I noticed some attractive, decorative chains on each corner of the house. They stemmed from the rooftop and ran directly down to the deck. I discovered that beyond adding to the décor, these chains also served a structural purpose.

Whenever it rained, the water on the roof, in what seemed an anomaly, would find its way to the chains. I was fascinated, watching water cascade down those chains in a lovely yet practical way. They never missed a beat or got off track. Gracefully the water made its way to the deck below.

The abundance of God's provision is raining down on His Bride. Because we are under the New Covenant, we live above and beyond the Malachi 3:10-12 mandate that states,

"Bring ye all the tithes into the storehouse, that there may be meat in mine house, and prove me now herewith, saith the Lord of hosts, if I will not open you the windows of heaven, and pour you out a blessing, that there shall not be room enough to receive it. And I will rebuke the devourer for your sakes, and he shall not destroy the fruits of your ground; neither shall your vine cast her fruit before the time in the field, saith the Lord of hosts. And, all nations shall call you blessed: for ye shall be a delightsome land, saith the Lord of hosts."

As you are obedient, heaven's showers will cascade down to everyone and everything connected to you.

You say, "that Scripture is about tithing?" Yes, it was, however, Malachi under the Old Covenant, addressed that statement as a rebuke to the people. Specifically, the resources we're using the provision of God to build their house, but not bringing the influx to build His house! In a sweet rebuke the generous heart of the Father also reminds them, that when you function under His canopy of blessing, not only will He have enough for His purposes, they will not be able to contain His outpouring and He will rebuke the devourer and preserve their influx, wherewith they will never lack. God dares them to test His provision.

He is the same yesterday, today and forever. Can you imagine taking the Father up on that promise? Tithing under the New Covenant is based on giving out of honor where all of the increase is the Lord and we ask Him how much we can keep. This falls under the order of Melchizedek rather than the order of Levi (see Hebrews 7:1-8:13). Take Him up on his blessing today, with the freedom of New Covenant.

James 1: 17-18 says that, "Every good and perfect gift is from above, coming down from the father of lights with whom is cast no shadow of turning." We cannot earn God's love nor His blessing because those gifts are based on covenant. The Father never breaks His covenant; test it.

We can be obedient people of faith and we can, over time, gain His trust and His friendship. Consistently, His favor follows. The point is, if the measure of God's blessing to us under the Old Covenant was extravagant simply for tithing; how much more lavish will it be for those considered sons and daughters, joint-heirs with Jesus? This opens the door to the "more than we can ask, think, or imagine" portion of inheritance currently being released. This is the season of *Shift* we have now entered into. An inheritance meant for every Believer, where the rain of God's glory cascades down to overflow!

The whole earth has been travailing and groaning to see the sons of God released and revealed; Romans 8:19-21. That time has finally arrived. In our obedience to the 'Garden Mandate' and giving honor to our Lord's eternal priesthood, **Shift—The transfer of wealth** will be loosed from heaven and manifested on the earth.

Have you prepared your heart and mind to steward His resources? Quietly and without fanfare, those who are ready are crossing paths and are coming together around creative ideas like, 'Cities of Refuge' and other Kingdom themes. The coming abundance of resources and influence will altogether rewrite your beliefs about giving. As individuals begin to experience this *Shift*, the opulence will prove so great that it will trickle down, bubble over and reach every single intended destination and recipient.

PROVISION FOR GENERATIONAL INHERITANCE

There are always a few teachers that capture your attention because you are either on the same wavelength, or their findings powerfully challenge your thinking. Arthur Burke brought forth such revelation in his teaching on *Leviathan*[1] that it rocked my world and uniquely transformed my thinking. Mentioned before, his insight on structural order of the Kingdom and expositions of the Bible, provoked me to look differently at the way I hear the Father and interpret His design for me. One key Burke presented was the difference between consumers and producers. For far too long, the Bride of Christ has leaned toward consuming and not looking ahead for the next generation. We are to produce much more than we use so there will always be a surplus.

> **Everything the Lord has structured requires personal investment and participation.**

In accordance to that thought, the *transfer of wealth* is not an entitlement for the Body of Christ. God has never created a welfare or dependency system. Everything the Lord has structured requires personal investment and participation. This transfer is not focused on the more we could gain. It is focused in every way, however, on the Father's provision for every believer to produce enough for the excess to continue multiplying for generations to come.

For some people, their passion is music and the sounds from heaven that no one has heard before. This sound was intended to bring change to the world. For others, it may be an innovative system creating efficiency for a business or multiple organizations. Others may have the gift of discovering the buried treasures deep within the earth. Whatever the genre, productivity lies within the expertise of the Holy Spirit, anointing you to create more than enough. This is what we call a plethora of wealth.

Many moves of God have been stifled by the nearsightedness of the leaders, living for today and not stewarding for the future. Hezekiah was looking at his own comfort, in 2 Kings 20:12-19 and desired only that judgment not come on Israel during *his* lifetime. This was safe, selfish and shallow. The Father has planned this transfer of wealth to continue and grow for many generations until all that He aspired for and wrote beforehand, in the strategy rooms of heaven, was completed. There should be no cessation or discontinuity between generations.

Walt Disney purportedly had tremendous foresight and well-laid plans in writing that which is still being carried out today at some level. Why is the Body of Christ taking up the rear when it comes to God's plans? It seems that the non-professing successes of our world often embrace and operate in God's provision, while the church sits waiting for the outpouring to find them! Today is the day to lead the way. Today we should be making plans for the future and following the mandate of Habakkuk 2:2 to, "Write down the revelation and make it plain on tablets so that a herald may run with it." To create something that will truly last, it is important to have the details and vision written down so it can be followed even after you no longer have an active role to play. This is not a complicated, scientific equation, but does involve very specific steps. Let's review them.

1. **Plan for the future**. Develop a strategy for the initial plan to expand and continue financially, spiritually and naturally. Leave room for flexible change, but stay the course of the initial vision.

2. **Spread the Wealth**. Set up a financial basis such as a trust or foundation; or even companies to produce in an ongoing measure.

3. **Choose participants.** Discern and confirm those people God brings to you to be a part of the overall plan you are called to participate in for His glory. Mentor and teach them to be able to replace you and to repeat the same for the next generation.

4. **Achieve Profitability.** Create a mutually beneficial, strategic alliance. This should be a collaboration of legal entities that together benefit and profit one another. Specifically, harness and leverage how participants can use the benefits of their structures and together enjoy greater increase.

YOUR PLAN WRITE IT DOWN

The book of Deuteronomy is a treasure of principles for business, life, and community, with an outline for a Godly and fulfilling life. Chapters 8, 11 and 28 are a profusion of non-optional standards that are universal and stipulate cause and effect. God set them in place to produce results, regardless of embracing Jesus Christ as Savior.

Take time to read those chapters in Deuteronomy again. They are not 'expired' truths because they are of the Old Testament.

Au contraire! When you live as a follower of Christ, He gives you legal jurisdiction to fulfill, and employ all the promises God has ever spoken. Romans 8:28 emphatically states that, "All things work together for the good to those who love God and are the called according to His purpose."

The Greek word Paul uses for the word 'purpose' is *"prothesis"* Which means the setting forth of a plan or proposal.[2]

A little understanding of Greek is required as we present 'prothesis' for your understanding. The prefix "pro" means "in advance" and "thesis" is interpreted as "a written down plan or strategy." If one carefully exegetes these two verses; Romans 8: 28 and 29, we will discover God's master plan for each of us. The pieces and experiences in our lives always come to a 'better end' as we march out God's written down and articulated plan. As we walk in the Spirit accordingly, the fulfillment of Deuteronomy follows.

Have you written down your plan? Have you brought it before God so he can expand it and disclose all that your vision might entail? Do you have relationships or mentors who can help you establish a plan worthy of eternity? Whether your plan is in place and needs expanding, or has been recently deposited in your heart and needs yet to be written down, Habakkuk 2:2 clearly gives you instruction to do so.

Business plans can feel overwhelming, but just answering the five questions relevant to any vision, is a good place to start: Who, What, When, Where, and How. Whether it's a promise Jesus has given to you, or a strategy to change world systems, it will not truly develop until you put it in written form.

Whether it's a promise or a strategy, it will not begin to develop until it's in written form.

When it's done, share it with someone. Surround yourself with those of similar heart and vision to sharpen your focus. This will help you achieve what assignment God has called you to manage. Assess and modify your plans often. Besides annual reviews, utilize prophetic intercessors and pray strategically for direction and needed changes.

Your calling is an organism; it moves, and morphs. It's essential that you continue to grow along with your Kingdom decree. This will make room in your life for the people God will bring to you for counsel. As you represent Christ to these new relationships, you will often find ideas for growth coming directly through His divine appointments.

Be attentive, listen, and wait for the transfer to become more evident in and through you. For sure followers of Christ will lead the way, opening economic doors and exposing people to the Kingdom of God. We will rewrite history.

Deborah has had God-given plans from the time she was a young adult. Together we have built business strategies and watched the Lord phenomenally morph them. We would invariably begin with a focus, but as we journeyed with the Lord in obedience, the full light of His design would dawn.

You must morph personally and professionally as Jesus takes you from one season to another. The goal is always to inherit the promise. Deuteronomy 28:13 reads, *"And the LORD shall make thee the head, and not the tail; and thou shalt be above only, and thou shalt not be beneath; if you hearken unto the commandments of the LORD thy God, which I command thee this day, to observe and to do them."*

In a picture frame in Deborah's office are two $5 bills along with that very scripture encased in it. A few years back when she lived in Redding, she was morphing her future plans again when a dear friend prophesied Deuteronomy 28:13 over her. It was confirmation of what the Lord had already begun to speak. Her friend first handed her a $5-dollar bill and then quickly gave her a second $5-dollar bill. When Deborah inquired of her rationale, the woman told her the Lord showed her such a downpour of abundance, that she wanted to receive a double portion for the seed she just planted. It was her last $10. Today, that picture frame serves as a daily reminder, when she walks into her office; remain focused and to stay the course. That was in 2004 and since then, the 'suddenlies' of God have visited her multiple times. Many of God's promises will come as a surprise and often materialize seemingly, out of nowhere.

Developing a life plan can be fun and imaginative and always flexible. Deborah reminds me that my life resembles the word He spoke to me back in 2008. God declared He could restore anything "in a day." I have always taken the Lord at His word, followed His plans and directives, and found much of my life was necessary formation for His next. Molting old skin and growing the new has prepared me yet again for the transfer I am experiencing today. God's plan has felt like a time-release event as we grow closer to Him. It's different for every one of us.

Pay close attention to your seasons. Watch for reoccurring patterns in your life. Jeremiah 29:11 reveals God's heart *"I know the thoughts (plans) I have toward you, says the Lord, thoughts of peace and not evil, to give you an expected end."* Many of you have embraced that promise for years. Some are experiencing fulfillment while others are patiently waiting. His promises are true, stay the course and "in a day," He will bring fulfillment, promotion, and advancement. It is time to look up. It's upon you.

SPREADING HIS WEALTH

Remember Chapter 4 regarding the *Storehouse Transfer*? The word wealth includes money, but far exceeds our limited Western

Those who have matured through the miles of testing, will walk in cadence with Jesus

definition. Wealth includes internal and external riches and power. An increase in capital is not cramming storehouses with more. An increase in *the* most important capital investment, you, is what paves the way for His mantle to be worn safely, prosperously and executed with divine intentions as you harmonize with God's heartbeat. Those who have matured through the miles of testing, will walk in cadence with Jesus as He expands their sphere(s) with power and authority, confident that increase will occur as they march forward.

The external benefits will flow seamlessly when the internal ethos is abounding. There are multiple ways to expand wealth in the natural. However you choose, make sure the basis of your business, idea, or investment is properly nurtured and legally protected. Without that, it is plausible that increase and expansion will not occur as He intended. Once your foundation is on solid ground, there will be room to create new avenues or diverse streams of income into the marketplace.

God will eventually bring new inroads with more opportunities to penetrate deeper into the culture. Thus, your sphere(s) of influence and dominion should expand, as will the wealth you receive from heaven.

An acquaintance of mine has started a water purification business in one of Africa's most troubled sectors. His business provides clean bottled water, bringing a health benefit to the country. It also creates income for that country, prospering the people of the land with financial blessing. This company is presenting Christ, discipling converts and sowing spiritual seed to transform that culture. As an added benefit, the connection in that country provides continual access for further business and Kingdom advancement. The abundance as described in Proverbs 13:22b, is demonstrated in living, spiritual, color within that nation.

If it can be done in one country, it can morph to fit the needs of any country. This extension is only one example of how to spread wealth by faithfully stewarding what the Father has given them. My friend is now a producer rather than a consumer for a needy nation. This gentleman's passion is to spread the fragrance of God is on the rise.

As you succeed in your current endeavor, consider including an expansion plan. Begin with the desires God has given you and ask Him how they may overlap into other areas of your life. Weigh His words and promises against your past experiences. You may find where you thought you lost your way, is exactly where He wanted to take you. Remember, God's wealth is intended to continue. Make sure you know where to plant a generational seed and how you propose to grow it. A King's responsibility is to spread the wealth and produce more than he consumes. This is a Kingdom purpose.

PARTNERSHIPS AND PROTÉGÉ

The Apprentice,[3] featuring Donald Trump, is fun to watch as it exposes the abilities and the motivations for success in the hearts of the participants. It only takes a little interaction to discover what excites contestants who want to enter the business world. Usually, it is all about the money and power that comes with it. This is not the Kingdom plan in any way, shape or form.

As you may have experienced, it is easy to become distracted from the real substance of wealth. It's more important to raise up and train a spiritual family that will carry on 'The Cause.' Be cautious as you develop leaders who you believe will carry out your goals and intentions. It can make or break the outcome if they transition in the wrong direction.

Even King David needed assistance from his leadership team during the last days of his life. Due to his poor planning, he needed to ensure the chosen heir was placed on the throne. This was important because the legal and logical heir was neither David's or God's choice.

Listen Kings, choose carefully who you bring into your business and who is chosen as the heir(s) in your stead. You must reproduce and reproduce with intention. Not everyone eligible on paper qualifies to fulfill the program He has given you for a generational inheritance.

Not everyone eligible on paper qualifies to fulfill the program He has given you for a generational inheritance.

What God is doing and how He is doing it, may defy traditions and even the reasoning of man. You are raising up protégé's—as a priestly King—and they must possess the Lords perspective with radical devotion to the heart of the Father. They must be teachable, with or without the right skill sets, and sit under your leadership as passionate pursuers of the heart of God. It's important for Kings to contain the glory of His presence as a leader in any business realm God places them.

As well, the apprentice should possess *your* heart to produce. That is taught, not caught. As a leader, it's imperative you implement measures to assess and determine foundational characteristics in one you would want to follow in your footsteps. You should outline key factors congruent within your written plan that can be followed in order to sustain what the Father is doing today. Be deliberate and decisive, raising up the next generation to carry the torch of your vision. You are not just a mentor. You are a son of God, training others who are called to be change agents under the mantle of Priest-King, and drawing others into the Kingdom. This is an essential component in the transfer, as God has determined it to be a generational outpouring.

PROFITABILITY: A MUTUAL ALLIANCE

Clearly, legal entities must be utilized to facilitate the structure of commerce, no matter what previous measures you may have been using. Among other things, the government has altered many of the benefits we enjoyed in the past, as they reach toward correcting the economic state. Knowing this, be sure to obtain legal and accounting advice. You do not need to know everything, but surround yourself with experienced professionals to give sound, guided advice. This will be of value to you as governments begin to restructure Non-Profit organizations. In their eyes, correcting an economic state may very well add taxes to the Non-Profit Corp, even remove or control political status and constitutional rights for the benefit of no-taxation.

Many times, it does not feel like a 'positive,' but more pressure to comply with the red tape of bureaucracy. However, we must live and work within the red tape of our new 'marketplace' as Kings and Priests come under one canopy. In order to take dominion, there must be a collaborative relationship between Kings and Priests.

The primary focus is to create and sustain the Master's possessions. This is not about who or how the tithe is spent. We established earlier that God always finances His plans. Speaking to both Priest and King, I would like to propose ideas for successful cooperation. To some this will not be new. To others, it will open up a bounty of opportunity to encounter God's provision.

501C(3) nonprofit organizations have been kept from the possibility of increase, as intended by the Father, due to limited understanding on non-profit revenue streams. Donations are fine, philanthropy is great and we know the tithe belongs to the Lord.

However, have you ever wondered why a Philanthropist's nonprofit organization has a seemingly, unending supply? Should these characteristics not belong to the house of God as well? Working in compliance with 501 © 3 corporate rules, it is true that the organization cannot 'own' a 'for-profit' entity. But a nonprofit organization can own shares of stock, units or royalties and share in the gain.

Equally there are benefits to the 'for-profit' corporation, as they can participate in that structural arrangement and further prosper. This is what I call a mutually beneficial alignment, both in the natural and spiritual. Such was the plan the Father gave me when we outlined the legal structural at Bethel Church in 1993 and built it accordingly. Today, there remains 'pads of land' that we built for business development as a co-laboring strategy to provide income for the church as well as the opportunity for business persons who wished to establish business opportunities on church property.

An important emphasis in proper stewardship of God's wealth — designed to last for generations —is creating permanent revenue streams for the operations and funding of Kingdom advancement. As Kings begin to receive creative ideas, new businesses evolve and wealth begins to grow. It is imperative that joint efforts of Kingly and Priestly duties cease being seen as 'us' versus 'them.'

Having personally repented and moved forward even while writing this book, I think it is time to execute some changes here and now. I believe the Father has already birthed this idea along with the necessary steps to execute it in the hearts of Kings. As well, He has introduced me to many Priests who have already begun to accomplish this in their community.

Joint efforts of Kingly and Priestly duties cease being seen as 'us' versus 'them.'

Yes, the nonprofit organization will have to pay tax on money made through a profitable company. This is called UBTI, Unrelated Business Taxable Income. Thus, a nonprofit corporation can develop revenue streams other than what the tithe was intended for, supporting the widows and the poor. These profitable streams can expand and support creative development of ministry *and* business.

Speaking to the Priest of traditional church structure, if you recall, Priests in the Old Testament often were involved in business! If you participate at any level of this *Shift*, it will be necessary to reinforce the foundation of your organization. Through a little legal and professional counsel, this is easily doable and essential. To see the *Shift* of God's authority established on the earth, personal flex and corporate change is required.

When I owned mortgage offices, I offered a franchise to a pastor friend as a secondary source of revenue stream for him. He became very frustrated for two reasons. One, he was not used to thinking about, nor had he ever had any training to execute business. Furthermore, he was worried endlessly about tax liabilities. I was saddened at the narrow-minded view he maintained.

If after his taxes were paid, and revenues proved greater than any pre-tax donation, then simply do as Jesus would do: render to Caesar what is Caesar's and rejoice in the abundance of God's provision. The mandate is yours, the provision comes from God.

Do not become stuck in the old wineskin when God graciously pours out the new wine upon your house. The Father has allowed us to participate in this *Shift.* It is now our goal within the nonprofit organization of '7 Degrees,' to walk out, exactly what we have talked about here. As a loving Father, He not only allowed us to participate, but we are honored to handle it as a son would and bring increase to the Father's house.

> **The *Shift* is bringing alignment to His Bride and God wants to include you.**

We have met many all over the nation that have heard the Father and carry the same heart. The *Shift* is bringing alignment and God wants to include you. Imagine the collaboration of Kings and Priests who will work together to build wealth for generations to come, regardless of governmental changes. Kingdom enterprise takes on a new look.

C H A P T E R   T W E L V E

DOMINION AUTHORITY

A DAILY MANDATE

When asked about "how to pray" Jesus responds in Matthew 6:9-13, with prayerful declarations that were to be spoken before the throne of God. These were not symbolic, but a literal two-stage connection with God that if employed daily would remind us why we are forging through territory He assigned to us.

Interestingly, in 1 Peter 2:5, this author who calls us 'a holy nation,' also refers to us being 'lively stones.' As living stones, we are never more 'in the moment' as when we are building a spiritual house. We are a spiritual house made up of living stones bonded together by the glue of God. Colossians 1:16 reads, "In Christ, all things are held together." This is a common prayer we are all quite familiar with, perhaps not realizing this was a template for daily triumph!

THE LORD'S PRAYER

Matthew 6: 9-13, is our guide on how to address the Father for daily dominion, not provision. Jesus, when addressing the motives of our heart, said, ". . . for your Father knoweth what things ye have need of, before ye ask him," (Matthew 6:8). We have confidence now knowing God is our provider. God has aligned His purpose in and through us. Therefore, we now declare that His purposes pervade over all our daily activities!

This two-part template is a direction given to us by Christ on how to build His house. At the same time Jesus directs the cadence by which we daily march to, as we occupy until He comes. This is a proclamation confirmed before the throne. Even as we speak, it is a growing anthem of victory, to take dominion in all things. Let us break it down.

PART ONE: REPRODUCING THE KINGDOM

Our Father which art in Heaven
Declaring our adoption, citizenship, and legal right to speak and move on God's behalf from His seat of government.

Hallowed be Thy Name
The proclamation of God's holiness wherever we labor. Confessing the spoken Word and with a heart of worship about His Glory; any honor given to us will bring Him the reward.

Thy Kingdom Come
Validating the mandate God gave us that we long to fulfill as we co-labor with Him to establish His government upon the earth.

Thy will be Done

Submitting to the Father's sovereignty over our lives while His purpose is evident in and through us, daily exemplified by the fruit of our choices.

On Earth as it is in Heaven

Yielding to become God's change agent and taking dominion at the same time releasing His authority where we occupy. This is a rooted truth that we need to grow in. God's will is already completed in Heaven.

Read this carefully. It has always been God's plan that the earth would emulate heaven. As the Kingdom of God grows from one person to another, influencing one city to another, profiting one business then another; His Kingdom will be established on earth in complete compliance with His will.

The second half of Jesus' prayer addresses daily attitudes and values as we remain in sync with the heart of God. This internal wealth must be embedded in our spirit so our natural responses produce the authority and resources needed. Out of intimacy, we remain free to operate from the truth of God's Word and there will be no loss of momentum as we increasingly take territories.

PART TWO: DAILY ATTITUDES TO SUSTAIN VICTORY

Give us this Day

According to Hebrews 4:7 God gives David a 'certain day; today.' One day at a time. Plans need to be made, but live with a focused heart full of God's presence every day.

Our Daily Bread

A daily dependence on the Father as He is our sustenance and our source. As noted in Matthew 6: 25-33, we are not to internalize nor stress over the needs in our life. We are to posture ourselves with anticipation that there will always be plentiful provision.

Forgive us our Sins

Acknowledging Christ's redemption brings freedoms we can enjoy. Atonement occurred in the intimate place of the temple. We also return to the inner chambers through communion and the remembrance of His gift connecting with the Godhead intimately, building relationship with them.

As we Forgive those who Sin against Us

Forgiveness is an internal activity of the heart that removes all barriers between the Father and one another. This is a daily triumph we humbly experience whenever we extend forgiveness and not judgment.

Lead us not into Temptation

Making no decision or action without consulting the wisdom of God. His wisdom protects us from the strategies of darkness, easily exposes temptation and keeps us from deadly distractions. 1 Corinthians 10:13 clearly states there is no temptation that He has not provided a way out from. Dependency on the Father keeps us close to His heart, providing us with daily instruction.

But Deliver us from Evil

The Holy Spirit will deliver us as we cannot always see what is coming our way. Not only can we apply and be covered by the armor of God, but we have angels to war on our behalf. The Holy Spirit lives within us, personally guiding every movement.

For Thine is the Kingdom and
the Power, and the Glory

An exclamation from a heart of gratitude and honor to bring Jesus a much due reward. It's His Heaven, His Earth, His Bride; and we are to daily bring Him increased glory, honor, power, and dominion.

Forever and Ever AMEN

There shall be no End! Isaiah 9: 6-7 reads, "For unto us a child is born, unto us a son is given: and the government shall be upon his shoulder: and his name shall be called Wonderful, Counselor, The Mighty God, The everlasting Father, and The Prince of Peace. Of the increase of his government and peace there shall be no end, upon the throne of David, and upon His kingdom, to order it, and to establish it with judgment and with justice from henceforth even forever. The zeal of the LORD of hosts will perform this."

The Father gives us an attainable vision and the ability to execute it through daily intimate fellowship with Him. With a personal heart assessment and alignment as directed in The Lord's Prayer, nothing can hinder the construction of His house or the joy of ethical abundance as we establish His Kingdom authority here on earth.

TRANSFER TO TRANSFORMATION

John Wesley, one of the leaders of the "the Second Great Awakening" in America, was asked on his deathbed, what he would leave as his final words to his family? His reply in a weakened condition was, "Nothing to do but save souls." Wesley then followed that with "Jesus loves me this I know." Now there was a man with a focus. Someone who knew why he was here and what He was to do with his life!

As we conclude our thoughts on the great *Shift* already in progress, I must bring home the greatest point I could make. God is uniquely equipping and empowering this generation to establish His Kingdom throughout our culture.

The result—without question—will draw people to know Jesus Christ as Lord and Savior, which will produce *transformation* everywhere we plant our feet.

The dictionary defines transformation as: a change in form, appearance, nature, or character; in essence, to change.[4] Our world is rapidly changing, caused by the spiraling conditions we are now experiencing. Our only hope is and will remain Jesus Christ and the presence of God who lives in and through us.

Although the ministries we may be a part of or associated with are doing their best from within the four walls of existing organizations, they still have little effect on our culture in general. As a matter of fact, there is an increase for those becoming de-churched, that means leaving the existing structure. The conversation rate is declining even more quickly. The story I have shared was not to bring discouragement, but to open our eyes to the larger need of the internal *Shift* that must occur within us individually as well as corporately.

With all the evangelistic efforts extended to reach the lost, specifically within other people groups, the body of Christ must lay down their differences, forgive one another and become in union with the purpose of Jesus Christ. Then we can reach the lost and disciple or raise up a generation to walk in fullness of His supply. In many regions, the dominant non-Christian culture waits for the crusades to end and after multitudes have confessed Christ, simply move in on them. In the after-wake of our evangelistic endeavors, they step in and take the spoils and the fruit of our labor.

False religions (cults/sects) understand how to 'occupy.' They recognize tenderized hearts hungry for change and establish relationships with vulnerable converts. They assist them financially in starting businesses to make significant impacts in their culture and families. Felt needs are met through relationships and the 'blind' assimilate into their cultural infrastructure. Eventually and inevitably they re-convert new Believers into their religious persuasion. They succeed because they lay down individual interest and in unity, with hands-on tactics, steal Jesus reward. This is exactly what the converging of Kings and Priests will accomplish if we can unify for His purpose, not ours.

The transfer of wealth has begun. As we align the King and the Priest like the pillars that hold the weight of the old Temple of God, the momentum will grow into an avalanche of souls that God's heart has longed for. This will not only bring the harvest, but will sustain it as we 'occupy' in and amongst cultural spheres and people God has given us to disciple.

The transfer of wealth has begun.

The open heaven I experienced as a full-time 'Priest' literally expanded to all areas of my life. In my current role as Priest *and* King, the evidence of an open heaven is revealed through healing, favor, position, and financial increase. God never ceases to amaze us! What once took months to accomplish, now often occurs in days. It is time to allow God's *Shift* to occur inside, around and through you.

Deborah and I position ourselves as both Priest and King and we declare our alignment is in place. We call forth the spirit of Kingship to rise up within you. We pronounce that the Mantle of Stewardship be laid upon your shoulders and you now walk in your correct role(s). We agree that the Father releases over you the wealth of His Kingdom to accomplish your assignments, that you may not only inherit your birthright, but establish it in accordance with His will as you take your position in the heavens as evidenced on the earth.

The storehouse of heaven is open and we assign your portion to be unleashed over everything you place your hands to do for Jesus. Collectively we stand in agreement; united as Apostles, Prophets, Evangelists, Priests, and Kings. We are now a force to be reckoned with. We declare from the mountaintops that by God's grace we will lay all the increase and all the glory at the feet of the King of Kings. "The Kingdoms of this world shall become the Kingdoms of His Christ." The wait is over. ***Shift: The Transfer of Wealth***!

ENDNOTES

CHAPTER 1

1. Proverbs 13:22b King James Version
2. John Dawson, *Taking Our Cities for God*, (Charisma House Publisher, 2002).

CHAPTER 2

1. Ed Silvoso, *Anointed for Business*, (Regal Books; from Gospel Light, 2009).

CHAPTER 3

1. Arthur Burk, "Garden Mandate" Plumbline Ministries, Whittier CA.
2. Ephesians 1:17-23, New International Version.

CHAPTER 4

1. *The New Strong's Exhaustive Concordance*, (Thomas Nelson Publisher, 1996) Hebrew #2428.
2. *The New Strong's Exhaustive Concordance*, (Thomas Nelson Publisher, 1996) Hebrew #2398.
3. *The New Strong's Exhaustive Concordance*, (Thomas Nelson Publisher, 1996) Hebrew # 6845.
4. *The New Strong's Exhaustive Concordance*, (Thomas Nelson Publisher, 1996) Hebrew #6662.

CHAPTER 5

1. *Webster's Dictionary*, Random House Publishers, 1972.

2. *60 Minutes* "Interview with John Boehner" CBS Broadcasting, 2010.

3. *USA Today*, Gannett Company, Volume 2, #4, 2009.

4. "Wall Street; Money Never Sleeps" Oliver Stone, Director 20th Century Fox, 2010.

5. Paul Bilheimer, *Destined for the throne*, (Bethany House Publishers,1979).

CHAPTER 6

1. *The New Strong's Exhaustive Concordance,* (Thomas Nelson Publisher, 1996) Hebrew #2756.

2. Pat Robertson, *The Secret Kingdom*, (Thomas Nelson Publisher, 1973).

3. *The New Strong's Exhaustive Concordance,* (Thomas Nelson Publisher, 1996) Hebrew #908.

CHAPTER 8

1. *Webster's Dictionary*, Random House Publishers, 1972.

2. Seth Godin, *Tribes*, (Portfolio Publishing 2009).

3. *Webster's Dictionary*, Random House Publishers 1972.

4. *Webster's Dictionary*, Random House Publishers 1972.

5. *Webster's Dictionary*, Random House Publishers 1972.

6. *The New Strong's Exhaustive Concordance,* (Thomas Nelson Publisher, 1996) Hebrew #7706.

CHAPTER 9

1. Os Hillman, "Two Pillars" *Today God is First*, Volume 2.

2. Paul Billheimer, *Destined for the Throne*, (Bethany House, 1979).

CHAPTER 10

1. Sebastian Junger, *The Perfect Storm* (W. W. Norton 1991).

2. *The New Strong's Exhaustive Concordance*, (Thomas Nelson Publisher, 1996) Hebrew #37.

3. *The New Strong's Exhaustive Concordance*, (Thomas Nelson Publisher, 1996) Hebrew #39.

4. H. Richard Niebuhr, *Christ and Culture* Torch books, 1976.

5. *Webster's Dictionary*, Random House Publishers 1972.

6. *The New Strong's Exhaustive Concordance*, (Thomas Nelson Publisher, 1996) Hebrew #4748.

7. *The New Strong's Exhaustive Concordance*, (Thomas Nelson Publisher, 1996) Hebrew #4053.

8. *The New Strong's Exhaustive Concordance*, (Thomas Nelson Publisher, 1996) Hebrew #1391.

CHAPTER 11

1. Arthur Burk, "Unspeakable Joy," Plumbline Ministries Whittier CA, 2010.

2. *The New Strong's Exhaustive Concordance*, (Thomas Nelson Publisher, 1996) Hebrew #4286.

3. "The Apprentice" ABC Television, Walt Disney CO, 2008.

4. *Webster's Dictionary*, Random House Publishers, 1972.

RAYMOND & DEBORAH LARSON
Living out the convergence of Priest and King

At the very core of this *Shift* is the expansion of Kingdom business and networks. The Larsons presently lead and direct both for-profit corporations and an independent 501 (c) 3 organization committed to global impact.

A passion for transformation has motivated the Larsons to successfully influence the area of Business through Consulting, Financial strategies and growth, Tax-Free Strategies, and Corporate Business Credit needed to be successful in any industry.

It was July of 2014, that Raymond and Deborah Larson were sent to Reno, NV, where the Lord had them establish a financial business to not only grow wealth, but to help clients sustain their increase and protect the principal.

Everett and Larson, independent agents focus on the client's needs, goals, and plans that maximize tax-deferred wealth and significantly minimize taxation.

In accordance with this *Shift*, decided to impact regions wealth in the natural and in the Spiritual realms.

At the same time, they have started a new work in 2016 involving the 501 (c) 3 organization. Their focus is

WWW.EVERETTANDLARSON.COM

Trauma Recovery, Counseling, Education and Community. Thus bringing freedom to those who have experience the sting and effects from traumatic events. This is a growing work changing people's lives. The Lord has given strategy to reach the lost with love as they Connect people to purpose through the work of 7 Degrees. After reading this book, you will understand His recent word to them: "I am going to do it again!"

If you are interested in attending classes, learning more about trauma recovery, participating in financial support or working directly with them, contact them at dlarson@7Degrees.org.

SPEAKER CONTACT & BUSINESS INFORMATION
DR. RAYMOND LARSON
DEBORAH LARSON

CONTACT THE LARSONS

Financial & Business Consulting:

www.EverettandLarson.com

 EVERETT & LARSON
FINANCIAL SERVICES

Non-Profit Contact:

www.RedeemingTrauma.com

www.7Degrees.org

www.Thegathering-Reno.org

7 DEGREES

The Gathering

Made in the USA
San Bernardino, CA
26 March 2019